Index

<u>Dedications</u>

I would like to dedicate this book to all the people that said I could and those same people that helped me achieve it.

Also to all the mutts and mutt lovers all over the world.

Introduction

I wrote this book based on the observations of working with many dogs and owners over many years.

Watching the behaviour and relationships between them and from my own experience with my best friends.

The essence of the book is what I have learnt over the years and to highlight the similarities in behaviour and more importantly what we can all learn to make our lives simpler by looking at how we treat and nurture our dogs. By putting it into simple analogies I hope to throw some light on these similarities and how we can use them in our lives, and our relationships human and K9.

Most of all I would like to introduce you to the friends I have had over the years and my story as a Security Dog Handler including the time around these anecdotes and hopefully give you an insight into the world of dogs and how they relate to us and vice versa.

I have made this possible by introducing to you my best friend Hooch who has been with me for many years and hopefully give you a view as to how much I value him and why, what he helped me achieve and the hurdles we have encountered and overcome together.

End Result

As the baiter took the longest short walk on to the training field in front of us, Hooch and I looked in his direction. I didn't envy him. A baiter is the man or woman that agitates your protection dog up and then in time takes the bite from the dog with a padded sleeve on.

It took some minerals to walk out in front of the spectators of a rifle club who are expecting a good show, but to also be confronted by Hooch, a 52kg Rotti x GSD.

Hooch's eyes wouldn't leave him; the passion behind them was only rivaled by the intensity of his stare. I have never been on the wrong end of that as he was my friend and was doing this to protect me. It was difficult to get him to show this level of intensity when play acting in training with me.

Hooch placed his feet; he knew what was happening next and knew he had to be ready. His balance was important, Hooch had to get a good start and so he placed his feet, wide apart and adopts his posture. Chest out, head levelled. He knew what was coming.

As soon as Hooch adopted this posture, I knew it was on and so I did much the same. Place my feet; get my balance right because he was a powerful dog with a lot of prey drive. I knew from experience, when that sleeve started moving Hooch would pull with all his strength wanting to cover the ground separating us and the baiter as quick as possible to hit him as hard as he could.

The baiter looked across the field and started walking diagonally to close down the distance. There was a distance that Hooch would see him as little threat and there would be a very clear line where Hooch would now take him seriously. It was important to judge it right because if he was too far away   Hooch would pay him little heed and the dramatics of the show would be lost, too close and Hooch wouldn't get speed up quick enough and though it would look good it would lose some of its spectacle.

We were here to impress, I had managed to get my company invited to put on a show at an exclusive rifle club in Bisley. We had to make it count and the only dog on the company that had the level of control necessary for off lead bite work which was most impressive, was Hooch.

So here we were, I wasn't used to performing in front of crowds and to be honest either was Hooch. But as the baiter shuffled towards us still about 30 feet away I felt Hooch begin to tense and pull forward. "Here we go" I thought.

The baiter was wearing his sleeve and walking with it in front of him like a knight going into battle, in the trailing hand was a starter pistol, he was going to fire it once on Hooch's approach and once when Hooch was attached and fighting.

The reason for the sleeve seems self-explanatory but just so you all understand, I have personally never taken a bite from a dog that rivalled Hooch's power in his jaw. I don't know if it was the cross and the Rotti power but it was painful even through the sleeve and he has made many a baiter drop to their knees or shout to get him off. Sleeve or no sleeve it hurt.

The starter pistol was to prove Hooch was gun tested and would bite through distractions and would only have the one focus.

I balanced myself and as the baiter walked closer he crossed the boundary and Hooch reacted. His hackles came up, he started pulling harder, begging to be set free. His growling started, deep in his throat at first, a guttural warning. His mouth opened slightly just enough to let the sound out. "Watch him" I whispered in a sharp tone and the sound erupted from Hooch's mouth. A deep powerful bark, he raised his lips to show his gleaming white K9's to prove he was serious. Spittle came from his mouth and he started bouncing on his front feet which exaggerated his look of impatience.

Every couple of barks he would throw me a look imploring me to let him go so he could do his job.

The baiter gave me the signal by raising his arm, I waited for Hooch to shimmy back and knew he was on the cusp of surging forward. I unclipped him so he could follow through with his momentum. He surged forward. It was times like this I couldn't help the smile on my face. Three or four years ago I couldn't have done this and either could Hooch.

I watched Hooch crash into the baiter and take the bite beautifully. In the centre of the sleeve and all the way to the back of his mouth. Crushing down to put as much power into his bite as he could.

His power and intensity was incredible for a dog that could come off the baiter and have a cuddle with you. He would switch on and off no problem and this was the beauty of Hooch. You could take him anywhere and send him in on anyone to bite them.

As he hit the baiter you could see in the baiter's face it was a good bite, it threw him off balance and he fired his second shot. Hooch didn't even flinch.

I called to Hooch to out, if you have ever been a baiter you understand. Once the dog has latched on even the smallest movement is painful because they have your arm gripped in 42 teeth.

Hooch let go and dropped back to the floor, he sat low on his rear haunches, looking like a missile about to launch back at the baiter. A deep low intermittent bark reminding the baiter to stay still.

5

I called Hooch back, he swung his head back quickly to look at me, I gesticulated and he backed up and turned around heading straight back to me with his tongue wallowing about. His expression gleeful.

 He came straight around to heel position as he had been taught and sat bolt upright ready for round two.

This is where Hooch and I were after many years of training and working together, we were at the pinnacle of our career. I didn't question whether he would or he wouldn't he didn't question whether I would be there right next to him. We had worked and trained together long enough to be a team. A team we were and still are.

 This is Hooch as the trained protection dog he came to be, this is the story of how we came to be this team and the friends I had on the journey to him. If you had asked me a few years prior I would have said this was the dream but here I was on a beautiful summers day on a training ground with spectators watching our every move and more to the point, Hooch not missing a beat. It was a struggle but we got there.

Well you've read what he can do, now you can read how we got there.

 This is Hooch at Bisley. He was around 6 years old at this time and still full of beans.

Why Dogs

Before I start I am going to add in a frame, you see there are many experts and trainers and behaviour experts that have made great names for themselves by doing great things.

Some of the training and socialisation I have done with Hooch has been wrong by accident, some has been right by accident, some has been right on purpose and some with the best intentions in the world has been wrong. But what I do know is this is the story of Hooch and I, and what we've done, been through to get where we are today.

Now, I know Hooch like the back of my hand, in the last nine years Hooch has changed a lot, so has the back of my hand. So yes he still surprises me but whether my methods were right or wrong, Hooch is a happy resilient solid dog, reliable, calm and well known to many people as a real legend. This is partly due to his breeding, natural temperament, but much of it is how we worked together and the training we did.

I have been lucky enough to continue with my love of dogs by offering a bit of training to people, family and friends. Because dogs fascinate me, but also because people fascinate me and the relationship and the cues dogs take from people.

It is all us, your dog will be what you want it to be. If you are conscious of what you want. When I help people with their dogs, I merely help them with themselves. I show them what their dog sees and what their dog takes notice of, that would be everything. Then I show them what messages their action/behaviours mean to the dog. Its a bit like common sense. Its simple but few possess it.

This isn't a training book, just an insight.

I have included snippets of a poem for a friend of mine Phil Nash, he and others have been great friends of mine. All of whom have helped supported and listened to me talk, and boy can I talk.

Phil sent me this poem a while ago and Phil knows why, every book needs a villain. The complete poem is at the back of the book if you want a sad moment.

In June of 2015 myself, my daughter and Hooch made a big move. Not to overdramatise it but it was a big move for us. We moved to an area where we

7

knew nobody and started a new life. Lauren had to find a job, I carried on working in London. But neither of us had any roots here.

I am not sure if it was the sense of freedom, the sea air or just the fact that I have lots of time on my hands that got me thinking about writing this book.

Since working with dogs I have wanted to put my pen to paper about all the similarities I see. Whether you watch people or watch dogs, or indeed both. With the help of this book I can help you understand people through the simplicity of dogs or dogs through the complexity of humans.

I am James and this is the story of my time as a Security Dog Handler and more pertinently the time I have spent with the dogs I have had the pleasure to work with.

It is an insight into how they influenced my life, how they adapted to life with me and my family and most importantly what I believe dogs can teach us if we just spend the time to understand the why and where for of their behaviour.

When I first started writing this book I found it very hard to decide on how to structure it. It is difficult to put my finger on what is important.

What my dogs have taught me, but without an end or a summary there is very little point to a start and middle.

Don't worry, their is an end and a point as you will find out.

I have written this because their is so much we can learn from our four legged friends and in some cases it doesn't have to be dogs. It can be nature as a whole.

Dogs are the easiest to concentrate on because they are domesticated and many of us come into contact with them and regularly observe their behaviour. But the point is do we see it or observe it.

I was a Security Dog Handler over many different sites and for many different people.

A Security Dog Handler is as the name suggests a security guard with a dog to protect himself. The fact that you are walking around with a dog eludes to the fact that these sites are more dangerous or there is more chance of running into trouble that a mere man couldn't deal with.

This isn't always the case. Sometimes the site is huge and its necessary to have a dog because they can sense things over a greater distance. It could be that the person you are working for or the site you are working at just needs a greater deterrent or just for status and the owners feeling of self importance.

I will go into this more later on in the book, for now it is suffice to say that these were my beginnings, little did I know that it would teach me so much about life and about many unrelated subjects.

My book will attempt to explain the meaning behind dogs behaviour as seen from my point of view. How this can be put into our lives with friends, staff and even children. It is all one big circle and I think some will be amazed at the simplicity of it all, and of course some knew all along. But whichever camp you are in it may be something you can use in everyday life.

The point is I learnt a lot from dogs and about dogs in this time and thought I would write a book and get it all down on paper for others to really learn the relationship and kind of a day in the life of a Dog Handler and his friends.

The harsh reality of dog ownership and the responsibility it entails.

Hooch is the dog that I worked with at the end of my career before leaving it to pursue other things. He is a big, handsome dog and I am asked so many questions about him and what he can do, how he was trained and a multitude of other questions. I thought at last I would write about how I came to have him, the work we did, the training, the challenges.

Not just Hooch but the dogs I had before and how my life led its way to Hooch and the experiences I had.

This is Hooch in his later years. He was around 10 years old when this picture was taken at a friend of mines while I was away for a weekend.

His wife is quite the photographer and many of the pictures in this book are done by Rachel.

I spent my childhood years scaring the life out of my parents at zoo's and taking too long on my paper round because a cat had hung around for a stroke. Many children did and still do because there is an affinity, an uncomplicated bond between children and animals.

To my family none of this love of nature will be a suprise. Though I blossomed late into working with dogs, I started when I was around 30, I'm pretty sure it was no suprise to anyone as I have spent my years marveling at how incredible nature is and what it means to different people and the reasons why.

As a child I wanted to join the police and become a dog handler. But with my capable mind and lazy outlook I came out of school with mediocre grades and have spent the rest of my life regretting it. You know what they say "youth is wasted on the young"

Nature is an incredibly complex but also amazingly simple thing. It means different things to different people but it always works. That is until us humans get involved anyway.

Nature is and always has been a large part of my enjoyment in life.

I find nature to be peaceful, uncompromising and honest. It would be great if the human race had kept some of these traits. Even the ruthlessness of nature is for the good of the pack or the environment and nature always has the courage of its convictions. Wether it see's, smells, or knows fear, the animal will still do what is best for it and its pack.

I'll never forget that quote in Jurassic Park. "Nature always finds a way."

You can read or watch a plethora of examples of animals being gentlemanly, protective, chivalrous, brave. All of these, if you were to analyse them and gave time to work out what that act meant to that animal you would realise it is just what they had to do. They just do it. There is no backing out or delegating. Animals have their job in the pack and that is all there is.

Wouldn't life be simple if that were true of us. When working nights at a large college I used to see deer regularly. It was lovely to think we were that close to nature that you could see these beautiful animals. Going about there business but very little got past them. They would graze gently in their little group as soon as you rounded a corner or came into view their ears would prick up and there sideward glance would focus on you. There was such beauty and serenity in them but also a power and strength.

In the early hours of one drizzly morning I was wandering along with Hooch and three deer wandered across in front of us, it was clearly mum, dad and little one. There is little as beautiful as seeing these creatures in the wild in the early hours, hardly any light and the little family are just wandering about finding fresh grazing. Seemingly happy and content. Their beautiful black eyes like moist black opals staring back at you unblinking. The perfect little family. They all knew we were there, in the dwindling light and the misty rain.

All three looked at us. Hooch and I stopped, I didn't want to spook them, not to mention the fact that inwardly I loved these moments. Where I felt that I was part of nature and getting to see things most people will never have the privilege of seeing. The male stopped in the middle of the road and just stood there. The other two disappeared into the undergrowth quietly and the male just stood, looking at me and Hooch. When mum and little one had enough of a head start he proudly walked into the woods and was enveloped by the dark.

You could say he was being chivalrous, brave. He was doing what males of his species do. That's all, he didn't turn up at mum and baby and brag or get told how awesome he was. Of course he didn't initially because he's a deer. But mainly because it means nothing to them. Its just what they do, no bells or whistles. Just what they do. I have had the privilege of seeing this many times since and it never fails to inspire me.

This wasn't why I got into working dogs but it was these moments that reinforced my want and love to be working around or with nature. The closest I could get to nature and animals was to do a job like this.

I had many jobs prior to this. None of them captured me, they really were for a paycheck only. Its difficult to keep my excitement up in roles that I didn't enjoy and I always saw myself in something more fulfilling to me.

The beauty that I found in working with dogs was there was always something more to learn. It put me together with like minded people who were interested in learning and working their dogs to their potential.

In the years I worked as a Dog handler I met people I still class as good friends though most of us have left the Dog Handling world.

It is a privilege to work with animals and to work at night. I watched the seasons change, I mean really watch the seasons and embrace all of them. The fresh crisp cold of the winter, the damp smell of the grass after a down pour. When it is so humid and you hope that during the night there will be a down pour so it can clear the air. The golden brown of the autumn as the forest floors become carpeted with the beautiful colours of the leaves as the trees discard their leaves ready for the new growth. It dawns on you slowly that nature works perfectly in the absence of any control or authority, nature just adapts perfectly.

In those years I probably saw more of nature than I will ever have the privilege to see again.

I saw more of peoples behaviour than I probably ever want to see again.

It is difficult to explain what dogs do. It is difficult to put it in words, I will explain why.

Everybody puts different values on different things, there are people who value their life and balance of work and leisure, others value work and the feeling that gives them. There are a million and one things people could value.

I can look at cars and have a longing for a big Chevy truck with an engine that you can count the revs like the beat of a drum. A big engine sounding beautiful that moves the entire truck when you rev it, so all the young people buzzing around in their Corsa's can hear what an engine should sound like. Hooch can be sat in the back with his doggles on looking like a hillbilly's dog.

You see when I start speaking about this, a passion ignites in me because it is my vision of the future. My vision includes all the special people in my life, living a relaxed life as an author maybe. But in a modest home with a Chevy on the drive for pottering about. Close enough to the sea to walk and with a nice view.

The reason this vision ignites a passion is because it is what I value in my life, a relaxed future doing what I love.

Many of you won't relate to the car, maybe won't relate to the author part or living by the sea.

The point I am trying to make is that it depends upon what you value in a friendship with a dog that will resonate with you.

I speak to people about their dogs when training them. Part of training as I will speak about is finding what the owners want from their dogs. It is only then you can start working with them, because just like children, staff, and friends every person expects and wants different behaviour.

I have seen managers with zero tolerance and I've seen managers take more disrespectful behaviour than I would from a close friend. *"We should each run our own race"*

So when asked what my dog means to me, I can go on for a long time. But ask me what dogs mean to the general population and I can generalise at best.

I have worked with many people who work dogs. For many of these a dog is a comrade, a friend, your best friend and he is a guardian too. He will always be by your side when many of what you would class as true friends have long since turned their back.

They will stand strong and many of my colleagues if asked to pick a picture of a dog. It would be a strong powerful looking dog stood proud next to him.

 If you looked on his phone or computer you would find loads of pictures of him cuddled or funny pictures of dogs wearing hats and glasses.

 If you asked a pet owning relative they would talk about cuddles, walks, and being good with the kids. Lots of pictures of their dog being silly or snoring after a long walk.

 So you see, for me to talk to you about what dogs mean to us owners. It would span from getting people out and about for fresh air and long walks keeping them fit. Working dogs and non working dogs at training for agility and scent work but secretly it is a social thing for them and a distraction maybe in a life that has too few distractions. People keep dogs because they feel safe with them in the house. They live on their own and want company.

This subject could fill this book up, there are so many reasons people have dogs and these reasons are hugely diverse, but they are all personal and are all based on what is of value in that persons life.

Every single person would tell you a different story of why and have a different need or want from their dog. This is the beauty of dogs behaviour. The dog will fill that gap, they will happily morph into or adapt to that role because that is what the pack desires and it fulfills his need to stay in the pack for food, comfort, and security.

So from a very young age I have wanted to work with animals. I find them fascinating, I find them as fascinating now as I did 30 years ago. The circle of life, their ruthlessness to ensure the pack lives on, the objectivity of animals cannot be faulted. All pack animals work, hunt and live for the good of the pack. I see so much in pack animals that I wish we as a race could morph into our society.

Many prominent figures have come up with ideas to control the masses and get us to all work together for the greater good. But they all involve control. Although with animals there is an element of control by pack leaders, the good of the pack runs through the pack. It is ingrained in their behaviour.

I don't know if the objectivity comes from a lack of emotion or an all encompassing need to ensure pack survival. But when I look into my dogs eyes I see emotion, maybe on a simpler level but it is there.

As for the need for survival of the pack, do you think us as humans have lost our way on that. We all have agendas whether it's materialism, status, arrogance. Some of our communities have a sense of entitlement. There are many things but we seem to have lost the need or want for the pack to survive.

I recall speaking to a co worker about some swans that had nested outside our work, when they hatched the swans left with all of the cygnets but one, for whatever reason they had left one behind in the nest. I'm guessing it was due to it being the runt or not being well enough to survive. My co worker said "I'll get him and take him to the swan sanctuary", now I will probably be lambasted for this but in my opinion I would have left the cygnet. I would have left him because it's the circle of life. An ill cygnet left in the nest is food for all types of scavengers or nature in general.   We disrupt the circle of nature by getting involved and trying to help. It may sound barbaric but this is how nature keeps itself alive, there is no waste because waste is used by other animals to keep them alive and to keep their pack living.

We as humans are the only animal that feel the need to disrupt the natural order of things.

Dogs still have this primal instinct along with other pack animals, we see it in dogs because they are so integral to all of our lives. Whether we have dogs or not we come into contact with them regularly.

Dogs have basic needs as we do, but we have many wants too, it's these wants and desires that lead us to do things that are counter productive to the greater good.

This is also why I love being around them, I don't want this book to turn into a mutual appreciation society of our dogs but an understanding of them. When I began to understand them over time I realised that in understanding them I also understood people.

Training and behaviour is easier with a dog, there is no grey area, it's black or white. Dogs like you or they don't. If they don't, there is a reason. *"If my dog doesn't like you, I probably shouldn't"* is one of my favourite sayings. I am not a crazy dog person but I believe in them because they don't lie. Not about the big stuff anyway. Trust me, if I forget I fed him and feed him again he will act like he hasn't eaten in a week.

The main thing I want to get across is that dogs can teach us so much, they are showing us things we never thought possible, sniffing out cancer, telling us when seizures are coming on, I watched an amazing program where two trainers took two dogs from a rescue home with a view to teaching them to become service dogs. The plan was to show to the world that with so many dogs in rescue centres the rescue dogs are an untapped resource and this would not only ease the the stress on rescue centres but would also give these dogs a chance of a great life with their minds and bodies stimulated and in a loving environment. So the trainers chose the two dogs and taught one to protect a woman with narcolepsy when she had a seizure so she would feel safer when out and give her confidence to leave the house knowing she was safe if she had a seizure. The other dog took the socks of a severely disabled girl and open doors for her to allow her a greater sense of independence and also to be her companion. The upshot of the programme was they managed to get these two lovely dogs to do these jobs for the people and allowing them confidence, freedom and companionship. What more could we want. They truly are our guardians helpers and more or less anything we want them to be.

This is why I would like you all to understand if you will allow me to show you what dogs mean, what they are capable of, and how we can learn to become better people, managers, business owners with the understanding of them.

The relationship between people and dogs has evolved but always at the heart of it is a mutual admiration and respect for what the other does best. Treated right we can be there best friends and vice versa. Also we can learn a lot from each other. The "dogged determination." To be in the moment and worry less about all of the material things us humans do. Dogs see everything as they see it, no agendas, no attachments, it's instinct and routine.

It's why humans continually explain their dogs emotions in human terms, because dogs have manipulated us, invaded our personal space by using their usefulness, cuteness, willingness to please.

They have had to do this to continually reaffirm their place in the human pack.

What I find really interesting is after working with dogs for several years, how many analogies can be drawn from dogs behaviour, how similar in fact we are.

I worked mainly with security/protection dogs so most of my analogies were based on aggression vs assertion. When I left the world of dogs and my boy became a pet, I found it astounding how quickly he morphed into his new role. Of course it shouldn't surprise me. Dogs have been adapting and flexing for their whole time with us, they've had to. But that is not to take away how incredibly dynamic, adaptive they are. I remember the day I got a "proper" job. I went to work really worried about how Hooch would adapt, how would it feel to him.

The day I got him when he was a year old he came to work that night and probably nearly every night since for seven years. Then one day, dad, (I'm not his biological father) goes off to work leaving him, even worse, I went to a Hotel for a week training.. I was so worried, would he be ok, would he cope, would he get let out enough by my daughter would he get enough walks. My daughter teased me on most messages or phone calls. First thing I would say is how is Hooch, she would reply "he's fine, I'm fine too"

Of course he would, and he did. It wasn't a huge stumbling block. We used to spend a lot of time training and walking, now he spent his days lounging, nothing more than moving from settee to floor and back and eagerly awaiting my return so he could go and terrorise the other dogs at the park and woods.

I guess what I am trying to get at is that whether it is people or dogs the thought process is very much the same. Good experiences can be revisited in our minds to teach us to get over fears and phobias. For example if presentations are hard for you, you can use a distraction. It takes the focus from you and as such gives you the space to present what you want to. I believe this happens with people who use flip charts, power points it all makes it easier to present because the focus is away from you. After one good experience you can then reflect on that

18

good experience almost as a crutch for your next presentation. The more good experiences means your confidence raises and slowly you build up that confidence. It allows you to hone your skills. I remember training with a gentleman by the name of Mick Tustain, he was probably one of the most influential trainers I worked with. He thought around dogs, he did things that were completely unrelated to what we were doing to promote a behaviour that we wanted.

As an example, he had a dog in for training that wouldn't bite a sleeve. He looked like he would, he gave it all the teeth and spit that you would expect. But on the run up to the sleeve he would bottle it, it wasn't a nerve thing and we couldn't work out why he was doing it unless maybe a painful bite once had put him off. Mick put a load of jumps on the run up, so the dog would jump, jump, jump and then the baiter (guy to take the bite) would be at the end of the course. Given no time to think, he did what came instinctively and done it well, the bite was great, he won the sleeve walked around with it like a trophy and all of a sudden biting was a positive experience.

Dogs don't think much past the last experience in the first instance. With this we were able after a few more goes to take the jumps away and concentrate on reinforcing the positive, subduing the negative. We changed the association behind bite work.

As a comparison, to really show what I am trying to get at in this book, I hate presenting. Should I say, I hated presenting. I did it in my work in front of customers and was fine with it, I could do it in my head. In fact my presentations, subject matters, body language and jokes were brilliant in my head.

But as soon as I stood up and was the focus of attention. Well, I fell apart. My throat would close up just in anticipation. Before I even got up I was shaking. I did it at networking meetings where I would have a minute. People said "you'll get better" and I did. I got better at failing. I knew when I was going to choke up and sat down first.

A while ago I joined another networking group. Same thing happened, just compounded my hate for it.

In a completely unrelated chat a gentleman at one of these meetings said, you need to hold up some pictures of end results to really show your business off and explain to the group what the scope of the business is. People were getting the wrong end of the stick. So I did.

I was doing it purely to show my business remit. The bi product of this was I concentrated on describing the pictures and explaining what I was doing. It didn't solve it, but it took my focus away from my nerves long enough to do an average

19

pitch. But, the long term effect was it gave me a positive experience to focus on in the future, just like the dog in my example. I took away the focus on what was bothering me and then when that worked I reflected on the good experience.

With dogs, the more good experiences they have the better. They become bomb proof. Even if Hooch has a set back he comes back from it. Because the confidence he has is ingrained in his mind. He actually thinks he is King Kong.

This is just one example, it is no coincidence that when I come up with analogies about people I tend to explain in a dog matter and vice versa.

It is all about positive and negative motivation. If you reinforce the positive it subdues the negative.

Sounds simple but how many of us do it with our dogs, or even our children, workmates.

I have had the unfortunate opportunity to do a lot of role play in my day job. I hate it, not only do I hate it. I see no point to it. I am sorry if this offends people that believe it's a good thing. I just see nothing in it. At best it's completely unrealistic and at worst it humiliates and forces a negative association into peoples minds making them fear it every time it comes up.

Yet still the people organising it try and play it up, rename it as practice as if any negative connotations disappear with a name change.

It will never be a good thing until the person doing it succeeds at it and has a positive to reflect on. As long as the person doing the role play receives criticism at the end it will never be a good thing in his mind. *"Common sense isn't that common"*

It has been a belief of mine for many many years that we have only just scratched the surface of what dogs can tell us, show us and do for us. But my learning is in their behaviour more than their practicality.

All dogs have the potential to be amazing. It's only us that hold them back. The joy of dogs is their simplicity.

This book started out as a book to aid people in management of people, using dogs as an analogy and the way they think, are trained and socialised. It is all about simplicity.

But the more into it I got I realised that the itch I really wanted to scratch was the relationships with dogs I have and many dog owners have. The way it enriches your life in many ways and most of all I guess was to pay homage to one very special dog that I have had the pleasure of bringing up from a year or so old. That is what I would like to share with you, the simplicity in their problem solving and more importantly how you can use that simplicity but that is another book.

For now I am going to impart to you my life and Hooch's life and how he became my friend, guardian and just an all round legend.

As I was saying, we can learn a lot from all animals but because dogs have been socialised and their lives are so integral to ours it means we can really see some human traits. Frans De Waal a primatologist summed it up,

"I've argued that many of what philosophers call moral sentiments can be seen in other species. In chimpanzees and other animals you see examples of sympathy, empathy, reciprocity, a willingness to follows octal rules. Dogs are a good example of a species that have and obey social rules; that's why we like them so much, even though they're large carnivores."

The way dogs work is just like children. When children fall over, if you give too much credence to it they will play on it and it will only get worse, pick them up and dust them off and they forget in milliseconds. It is no different with our dog family, I can't tell you how much time I spend trying to convince customers and friends with rescue dogs. Don't concentrate on their past. They won't if you don't, yet all their misgivings are explained away by the treatment they have received in the past.

A lot of rescue dogs have endured an awful beginning, they are the lucky ones really. Many are enduring this cruelty as we speak. Though their pasts may be true and would go a long way to explain probably all of their behaviours, the longer you dwell on the negative the more it will become part of the dogs identity. Similar to people again.

It's the same in society today, the atrocities some people commit and the poor behaviours are explained away by a poor upbringing or wrong decisions. While all this is true and I have sympathy for these people you make a choice, are these poor decisions or situations inflicted on me going to define my life, or am I going to break the cycle.

Unlike dogs it is a harder and braver thing to do for us, because we have a higher level of thought process. Dogs will just overcome given the right training, socialising and not being made to relive abuse by owners who constantly Molly coddle or change their own behaviours to counteract how they think the dog will react.

We mustn't keep excusing people's bad behaviour because of their past. Although Chaplin said *"we are the sum of our past experiences"* doesn't mean we have carte blanche to behave badly or allow these things to obstruct or hinder our lives. We are indeed *"the sum of our past experience"* but we have a choice

21

wether we choose to allow that to help us grow or to wither in a storm of emotion where there are no winners.

As a friend used to say to me, *"we all have our own story."* Use that story like so many influential people do to strengthen yourself, not as an excuse so people pity you or excuse your bad behaviour.

If you want an example, look at the Internet for tear provoking stories of dogs who have been abused to the point of near death and then become happy, friendly socialised dogs that have let go of all their baggage and moved on with it. I know they can do this in part due to their instinctive need for survival but surely if we dig deep we can also use this to our advantage and really move on with our lives in a positive manner.

If we were able to look at problems that are relevant to this moment. I am not going to take anything away from people who have endured a bad start, but we can learn how to overcome our past and become who we want to be despite what has happened to us. Using and gaining strength from the fact that nothing can hold us down. We have all been through things that have been less than perfect and sometimes downright diabolical. But it is within us to rise from all of this because it is within us to rise back up. We to have a survival instinct.

Its all about putting things in perspective and trying to remind ourselves of what we can influence and change and what we are just wasting our energy on.

This is how dogs do it, there couldn't be a more nonchalant animal I swear, a better symbolism for "whatever." Hence using dogs as an analogy.

The beauty of dogs is that we all embrace the same training methods with children and colleagues as we use for dogs. It sounds simplistic and it is. But it is also true.

Its simple and we use it all the time but because the reward is different many of us separate it. If you were to say to your child "clean your room and I'll take you to the cinema" or to a colleague "could you stay on for an hour and I will pay you double for the hour." Or even more subtly, if you were to imply to a colleague that by taking a course or completing a course of action would help in their achievement of a promotion. This is all reward motivation, whether it is implied, said, or offered visually. It doesn't matter. It is exactly the same thing. It is also the same as saying "sit" and offering a bit of hot dog to your pet.

The only difference is memory. You can't ask a dog to do what you want it to do with the promise of a treat in the future. Trust me it doesn't work like that.

You can bring this to nearly anything you want in human life. Kids, work, customers.

As I will speak about there are very few altruistic people. Also in the same way as humans the more positive experiences you give a dog. Such as treats when training, or indeed a lack of treats when they are not doing it right. They get the hang of it and no longer need treats. The association becomes enjoyment and no longer centred on the treats. This is why in training you can use treats for a while and then as you cut them down the dogs enjoyment of training doesn't become less because in thier minds they still have the association of enjoyment linked to the exercise.

For example I have not given Hooch treats for training for a very long time but he still gets excited when we do training because in the same way Pavlov's dogs salivated when the bell rang so do dogs continue exhibiting their trained behaviour because the outcome has always been favourable for them.

Some call it lure training, reward motivation. I just think it is training without conflict. In the same way you don't allow a child to expect these treats, you don't do it all the time but because you do it some of the time the child, work colleague subconciously learns the game.

If you were to always treat they would then learn to expect it always and it loses its edge. I don't walk my dog with an inexhaustible supply of hot dog, every time he is in the right place feed him again. He would be the size of a house but I tell him he is being good. Give him a stroke to assure him he is doing the right thing. At first I used treats but as he learnt I gave him less and less but I always told him he was a good boy when I rewarded him. Now the praise is a reward because it is associated with a treat.

In the same way as you would be bankrupt if you offered your young one a trip to the cinema every time they tidy. But they also have a positive association and from time to time you reinforce it by giving them the reward. It is really the association with good behaviour and reinforcing it by saying this is the way to behave and for this you get good things.

It is funny because it starts as a bribe in simple terms and ends teaching life lessons. You want good things you do good things and they will come.

In exactly the same way people find the same operant conditioning works for us. As an example I used to help run a Security business. We had an operations manager who organised all the staff. I looked after all the admin and training. When we were short of staff and really up against it the ops manager used to ring around and try and strong arm people into working for us.

So imagine, as we Dog Handlers would regularly do,sat in the night or the early hours of the morning. Maybe sat in your car or as I used to, sat on the bonnet looking out over the site you are working on. Sites vary a lot, you could have

23

been sat soaking wet or covered in mud or maybe you are on a lovely clean site. You've got the privilege of another 12 hours of walking around in the cold and possibly wet. Your phone rings and it is the ops manager. The only time he ever rings is to get you to do more hours. You know when you say no, he will try and strong arm you to work. You are now answering the phone because you have to, he may have information relevant to your shift or site. In your mind you know it will probably be to work more hours. All you have to do is think of an excuse. We've all done it. You answer the phone acting like you've got the hump. Argument with the wife, not feeling well, all in the hope that knowing you're not 100% he won't even ask. He probably still will because covering shifts due to sickness or absence is usually a very desperate measure.

I'm accused of overthinking way too much. But how about another scenario.

How about I ring, I am the friendly one. I don't strong arm people. Never have because it wasn't part of my job. I used to ring to see how the staff were. See if they needed anything. Talk about training, when the next session was or book in 1 2 1 training for them to overcome challenges that needed more focus. The member of staff would answer the phone happy, positive. At the very least they wouldn't have had a chance to make an excuse up.

Its all the same process. Negative association, positive association. Be careful what association people put to your phone calls or meetings.

It is exactly the same as working out how to manage people. It is about setting yourself up with the best chance of success and how does that look. Take a moment to work out when is best to ring or take that person aside, who is the best person to have the conversation. It works for people as it does for dogs.

I have had many customers over the years who have been manipulated by their dogs. It usually comes in the guise of human emotion. Let me explain.

I go to see people with dogs, separation anxiety is a problem with many. *"Fido misses me so much, he howls all the time I'm out."*

To say your dog misses you is putting a human emotion to your pet. The truth in many cases is as simple as this. You are part of their pack and they haven't allowed you to leave. I'm afraid it's true.

When they come and hug you as they do when you are unhappy or not feeling well. In many cases this is born of affection and you can look up many stories where animals build an almost instant affinity with people who are ill or disabled in some way. I believe this is also born of the animals need to comfort and I also believe that animals, mainly dogs because of their closeness to us have this amazing power to fortify us in our times of need. It is in these moments truly altruistic in my opinion because there is nothing to be gained by them. Maybe it is just their pack instinct but in my mind I like to think they have an amazing closeness and want to please us.

I have watched many programs and clips of what dogs can mean to people and I belive in these moments the dog feels the same as the person in their hearts but I also know from my own experience it is a simpler form of emotion, a more honest form of emotion.

As a testament to this, there are Pets as Therapy dogs. It is a fact that having dogs around can aid in rehabilitation, and reduce stress. I always wanted Hooch to do this but unfortunately his tail would be a hazard in a hospital or hospice.

I watched a program once where they piloted a scheme in an American Jail where the inmates had to train dogs from a rescue centre. It worked so well, They had to get them to a standard of training where they could be rehomed outside of the jail. So they trained them in good manners and basic obedience. It was a massive success and at the end of the programme the titles said that the prison continued to offer this course.

The amazing thing was, the inmates had such a bond with these dogs that anti social behaviour dropped, the inmates testified to their lower stress levels, and general feeling of well being went up. Now you could explain this away with the reasoning that they now had a productive distraction. But add this to the scientific fact that they bring stress levels down, is it any suprise it was a success. I also think that part of the draw of these people to dogs is there honesty.

You don't need to second guess dogs, they just are what they are and they see who you are deep down. There is no stress within your bond to your dog as long as you know how to treat and respect them, that's it. They will be honest with you and for many of these people in prisons, by the nature of where they are they have spent a long time in friendships, relationships that are subject to threat. Whether that be physical violence, mental cruelty, or just running from authorities. The relief of a relationship with an animal that is stress free, based on nothing but honesty and a desire to accept each other for the friend they are and that's it. It goes back to my earlier point, dogs don't need you to have money or possesions. More importantly for this example is they don't judge or care about your past. What a relief for these people that have possibly been judged most of their lives and certainly the ones that regret it and want to change. This may be the first friend they ever have that has looked past their crimes and behaviour.

People talk about dogs and their honesty but honesty is a tricky subject, mainly because it is subjective. You see my dog is honest in my mind, However dogs can manipulate, which is classed as a sinister word, dishonest word. To "manipulate" is to handle or control in a skilful manner. It has long been classed as a dirty word. It isn't. Our dogs manipulate us all the time with their PDSA faces when you're eating or acting sad when you're getting ready to go out.

Do you want to know who the greatest manipulators are? Children. From the age of 0 they can do it. Physically they are born to tug on heart strings.

Look at Disney characters, it isn't a coincidence that the cute Disney characters have features that wouldn't look out of place on a baby or a puppy. These are purposeful animations to promote a response. It isn't a shock that all the baddies are are drawn in one way, sharp features to make them look sneaky and sinister. All the cute, good characters that Disney want a favourable response too have round faces and big eyes perfectly set.

Children are born ready to manipulate parents and anyone else available to pick them up, feed them, change them, give them attention. My daughters are 17 & 19 and sometimes I walk away from conversations thinking, " *I have just been mugged*" Its true. Its not sinister or evil. It is life, nature.

Dogs do the same but because of their more simple thought process they don't use it to deceive and they are genuine as are kids. It is black and white for them all. They want to obtain something so they use their features or actions to get it.

Dogs can turn the charm on just as children can. People who own dogs, or many domestic animals for that matter know how to use their body language to illicit a response from us.

It may be looking cute, it may be testing your patience but it is all manipulation.

We all manipulate, more than we would like to admit too.

But the basic honesty of a dog is part of my love for them. Also if they are looking sad because they want a treat, it is much simpler to identify than people who are after something.

I believe this is all due to the simplicity of their needs.

I guess what I am trying to say is that in the main you can only trust young children and dogs to have simple agendas and agendas that are born only of their survival and to establish their place in the pack.

Part of my motivation to write this book was because I was lucky, all of my dogs have adapted into the family environment, it's all about confidence and in this book we will talk about confidence a lot.

Confidence is probably the single most important characteristic we can help to instill into our dogs. It's the same for us humans. If you dash your childrens hopes at a young age and continue to do it. You may class it as a reality check. *"Just getting them ready for the real world."*

You have a shock coming. Not only are you not arming your children for the real world. You will destroy them inside.

Just like dogs, children need confidence too. I believe it is important to teach everyone and every dog and look at the gifts/talents they have. Not try and get them to do what they clearly can't. The important part is the balance.

Kids shouldn't think the world is all Unicorns and rainbows but they need to have the belief in themselves to try new things and be open to new experiences always with a healthy respect and an appreciation for their new experience.

I wouldn't look to a dog like a Spaniel to look after me as a protection dog, you look to a dog that has propensity to violence and the confidence to carry it out. If I wanted to find something, a Spaniel all day long. If you want a picture painted hire an artist.

It is the same with children, some kids just excel at other things, go with it. Look to their strengths because their strengths are probably born of enjoyment and surely that is the way to go. If we could all fulfill a life doing what we enjoy. Wouldn't that be a wonderful world. Wouldn't it be nice to instill in our children and our work mates the confidence to try new things, to ensure them that failure is just a notch on the compass of where not to go next. This way their confidence builds and when they do find what they enjoy they can pursue it with no judgement.

Confidence is what makes us, us. Not arrogance or overconfidence because that can be born of lack of confidence. What we show on the outside with bravado is rarely what we have on the inside.

Confidence can be gained at any time during life. With us as it can be with dogs. As per my earlier example with presentations. If you have good experiences even after several bad ones you can prove to yourself you can do it and hang on to that.

You can tell with dogs, children and members of staff for that matter. You just have to be looking. Many of us are too busy to look, I mean really look and take in what is happening. Why are they avoiding certain activities. Why are they defensive, moody. It doesn't take a lot to see the signals especially in children and dogs. As we get older we learn how to mask a lot of our reactions but you can never fully mask them because again it is instinctive. Dogs have never learnt nor tried to learn to mask them so they are very transparent.

27

Dogs can't help but show exactly how they feel, it exhibits itself in many ways but because dogs communicate instinctively they are easier to read than people. You see dogs have no hidden agenda, no ego. They have instinct, this instinct leads them to do what they do with no or very little thought process.

I am talking about situations that happen, not training and controlled environments. If a dog wants to play with another dog, it will attempt to play with that dog. The other dog could be baring its teeth acting aggressively but all that is on that dogs mind is play.

Same as a submissive dog may well still be attacked by an aggressive dog, because they work on impulse, this is why confidence plays such a huge role in their lives.

A dog needs to be balanced and to be balanced it needs the confidence to go about its normal business with no worries. It's the same as people.

Children need the same level of confidence because we all know as we get older that to walk into a party or a job interview other people are judging, weighing up. It is no different than the pack hierarchy of the dog pack.

All is weighed up very quickly, we learn this as we get older and whether we have it or not we learn to emulate confidence so we are received seriously and the pack respects us immediately. Wouldn't it be wonderful if we could instill this in our children from a young age so that they do this with no pretence. The confidence is theirs not just a mask they wear. It would stand them in good stead for life. It is all pack dynamics, lets not fool ourselves. It is no different.

I know I need to explain this further because for our brains that have been subjected to social construction from the day of our birth, we may find it hard to understand that what a dog does isn't altruistic, just as most good things people do isn't.

What I mean is a lot of people do what they do, good or bad because it gives them a sense of wellbeing in their hearts, or heads. Depending what school of thought you subscribe to.

It doesn't mean it's any less good. It is selfless and people do things via instinct, a goodness that they have inside of them. But they do get something out of it, wellbeing, a good conscious, that feeling of warmth when you give a beggar a sandwich, when you donate to charity. I promise you this isn't cynicism. Those wonderful people balance the world with their great deeds.

However it is not selfless in the true definition of the word. Same as dogs but in a slightly different way. You see to a dog it's all about the pack, there is nothing else. Survival of the pack at any price. I couldn't tell you how many people in the security dog world said "*this dog would die for me*" of course it will, you are its pack, or its yours.

That's excluding the fact that a dog has no understanding of life and death, it only has pack and the survival of its pack. It makes its deed no less brave but I believe it's important to understand the motivation, to understand this is to understand how to use its assets and behaviours best.

Firemen are a good analogy, firemen are to be admired and it's certainly not something I would undertake, but do they do what they do through selfless bravery or is it an ingrained need for the survival of their pack/race that spurs them, a selfless bravery that only exists in some of us or is it really that they are selfless heroes that just do it because it needs to be done. Is it the rest of us that have lost something in our evolution that these select people have maintained despite us.

This leads me on to my point. Dogs think the same way we did, when we were primitive, before we were corrupted by the need for material things and desires of things we couldn't or can't have. We place a value on everything. If the value is high enough we as a race will do nearly anything to obtain it.

These needs and wants are different for everybody and the values change depending on the individual. This is similar to the dog world, and also it has a bearing in life.

When I first start training a dog, the very first thing you need to instill in your dog and work out from your dog is value, what is the value of things, what does the dog value, ball? Treat? Me? All of these things have a value and the basic rule for a dog is if it has value in something, it will be led by the person who is that valued item or controls that valued item. If your dog spies another dog from across the park, will he/she go and see it? It depends, is what you are doing with your dog at that moment more valuable than playing with that dog.

What about your children, what do they value. You should know this. Many times it isn't what you think. Many times it is your time and attention but in the absence of this it is Xbox and Playstation. Only in your absence though.

If you buy your child a ball the only time your child can really have fun with it is if they interact with you or their siblings and friends. But if you were to buy them a games console you lose that interaction but you also are of little value to them because they can have fun on their own now.

Of course the value children see in things has been dictated by you through their formative years.

For Hooch it was playing ball. He could ignore anything as long as the ball kept being thrown. For other dogs its food, or a toy etc. But in all cases it must be what the dog values.

It is part of a dogs training to find what they value and use it for their training, to use it as a lure to get them to understand what you want from them and then to supply them with what they value as their reward.

People are the same, you might think that by paying a premium for staff you will always obtain and retain the best staff. But if the member of staff puts more value in his quality of life, job satisfaction, job title and status, perks, work environment then you are not playing to his tune and although by hiking the money up may retain him for longer it won't keep him forever, he may just want development or respect and acknowledgement for doing a great job.

You must always feed your staff with what they value if you want to retain them. Working out what they value isn't even hard but seems to get missed regularly in the people I speak to. You only need to ask them, things like acknowledgment should really be a natural thing for us.

When you are teaching your dog to heel, you can tell a dog when it's in the wrong place as much as you like. You can continue to tell it where not to be, but until you tell it where it should be you will always have conflict.

Same with people. You can continually tell them the bad job they've done, what they shouldn't have done but you will always have conflict until you start telling them what is expected of them.

It may sound daft and basic but how many of you are agreeing now in your heads and thinking of times when you've missed this vital step.

Because unlike dogs who have nothing else to do but to think simply, we as business owners, parents, employees, friends, wedding goers, shoppers, car and house buyers, private landlords, book writers, readers, cooks, maids, gardeners etc, we are all we to busy living by the social confines of a normal life to drop back into *"primitive thinking"* and just take a step back and look at the simple way.

I remember years ago when I rehomed Hooch, he hated the kennel. In my mind the kennel isn't necessarily where I want my dog to be, but when you are working and have kids in the house it gives a dog quiet time to have dinner and relax after 12 hours of work. They can sleep, relax in the fresh air without children hugging them and playing, when you take them to work they are increasingly tired through your working week.

So a kennel is the answer.For Hooch it wasn't the answer he was looking for. So every morning I took him to the kennel and every morning I sumo wrestled with him to get him to stay in the kennel. Then one day I had a brain wave.

How simple would it be to put his dinner in their? Let him walk in and whilst eating dinner I would without a fuss leave and bolt the door. Simple, so it turned into a routine, but a routine with a positive outcome for him and me. Step back from the problem, conflict is a loss. There must be an easier way around it. There is always an easier way. I go slightly deeper into that story later.

So once again, in many many ways working with dogs taught me how to resolve conflict, effectively and easily.

Many people say if you allow an interaction to result in a conflict you have lost. It is true and no more so for animals. If a dog feels the need to fight, it has either been pushed so far it has no choice or it isn't balanced.

Pack leaders rarely fight because if a pack leader or any of its pack receive an injury in a fight, the pack is weaker. Instantly, this weakens the pack. If it is the pack leader, the up and coming pack leader has to step forward. In short it is counter productive, not good for the pack and therefore not something the pack or leader will entertain.

You can pick up books or type into the internet about pack leaders, but the easiest way to explain is that pack leaders are confident, strong and assertive leaders. Not barky, shouty dogs. Just like people, a doorman that gently asks you to leave and ushers you of the door. A doorman that shouts in your face is probably not a confident pack leader.

To keep a dog or a person happy and content and get the best out of them. Find out what they value and supply it in exchange for them doing the best job they can, Because you see dogs aren't fickle. They don't choose who or when and they have no understanding of material things, they only understand base instinct. Food, water, reproduction and who is heading up the pack.

If you are pack leader, if you are capable of being pack leader then you are for the good of the pack and that is all that matters.

Wouldn't it be lovely if we as humans were like that. Too often are we are judged on things that really matter none in the grand scheme of things, and the things that do matter take a back seat, respect, morals, leadership all these internal values and behaviours that we carry around mean nothing compared to how much your trainers or your phone cost. What an incredible world we live in.

When you look at it with perspective you can come to understand that in this day and age you can have people, celebrities who are morally and ethically bankrupt but because they have wealth they continue to make money, grab the headlines and live incredible lives which only fuels peoples adoration of them more.

Down the bottom of the pile working hard and just keeping their heads above water are some of the most switched on compassionate people of our times but nobody will listen to them because they don't dress right, go to the right clubs.

I am not talking about all celebrities but many are famous for nothing and some are even famous for how devoid they are of feeling, compassion and even intelligence in some of their cases.

It is an upside down world, and in these cases when you look closely I am sure you would agree the way of the Dog is by far the better path. To follow only those who are strong enough and brave enough and most importantly balanced enough to be followed.

The ones that are all of these things are calm, they aren't aggressive because that is counter productive. Ask anybody who knows what they are talking about with dogs many of my readers will agree.

An alpha dog or bitch, is calm, assertive and confident. They have belief in their leadership. It's the same with people. You all know pack leaders in your workplace, family and friends. It's just natures way of keeping everything in check and making sure that we survive. We would be useless without pack leaders and we are animals too.

A bit like that person that walks into a party and people gravitate too. Not the birthright, or the money, or the social connections. Just the person they are, the strength in mind that they have.

I worked for two very important and rich men in my career. One was a born leader, smart, charming, engaging. He was a rich man so his clothes were tailored. He had the stance the posture. You could have put him in a potato sack and he would still command men. The other was nearly as rich but you could have put him in a 50 grand suit and you would still have passed him in the street. It isn't money or birthright. It is a gift, maybe it is hereditary but it isn't something you can mimic.

The right person for the right position decided by the pack for the good of the pack.

Sounds like the politics of envy, it is in a way. I envy a simpler way where the people at the top and leading the pack are suitable to lead the pack for the good of the pack. In a way you could call it altruistic and selfless.

DOG HANDLING

The Journey

The story of Hooch really started a long time ago.

In 2002 or thereabouts, my memory is shocking for dates. I was lucky enough to be working for a prestige car manufacturer at their head office and had a great job, dogs and cars are my passion. Working with cars gave me an instant gratification.

My then wife left her employment and I was forced to find a job that would be more lucrative to support our family.

It did not make me happy, one day I was content and settled in a job I loved, next I was chasing the buck. I had to find a role that would offer me money right now.

The next couple of weeks changed the direction of my life in a profound way that has stayed with me and is the motivation behind this book. It turned out to be the best thing that ever happened to me, just shows you that you never know what the fates are weaving for us. So we might as well just go along with it because it may be the greatest lesson you have ever learnt.

I found a job role on the Job Centre website. It looked legit but it was hourly paid and as many hours as you wanted. But more than this it was a job and a role that I had wanted to do from a young age. A Security Dog Handler.

I rung the number on the application and was invited for an interview that week. I was very excited about all of this. A job that I had always wanted in such easy reach, I should always remember that nothing is that easy if it's worth having.

I had an interview with a guy who had his own company sub-contracting Dog Handlers for big estates.

A young man who to me knew what he was talking about, I knew nothing so as they say "*in the land of the blind, the one eyed man is king.*"

He told me what I needed to know (mostly), and my heart ruled my head. My affinity with animals had always been really strong and this was something I wanted to do from a really young age, a dream come true if you like. He offered me the job there and then. I was ecstatic, I couldn't wait to begin my new role as a Security Dog Handler. Something I had always wanted to do and felt I would enjoy this so much and it would pay me enough to support us. He told me I could come back in a couple of days and pick a dog from a kennels near him and as I had an estate car I was ready to go.

I remember getting home and ringing my Mum, I don't think she was over the moon. Nobody could know where this job could take me but my Mum has always favoured stability and security and self-employed doesn't offer you that. I was so excited and I didn't get much objection mainly I think because I was too excited to entertain anything could go wrong.

Now I know all you Dog handlers out there will be scoffing at me right now because this is how many dog handlers come into the profession.

All the gear no idea, but I was naïve and probably shouldn't have done it but I had such an emotional draw to it I said yes there and then. It would nearly double my salary in a role I had only ever dreamed of before.

So I went back a couple of days later to choose a dog.

I was confronted with four dogs, three GSD and one Rottweiler. George was the Rotti's name and I only had eyes for him. He was a handsome powerful looking dog with a beautiful coat and a powerful demeanour. He put the others to shame with his beautiful black and tan coat that shone like a newly groomed show horse. His coat felt like silk and I remember wondering how you get such a shine on a dogs coat. His muscles looked powerful and his stance was one of confidence and from the very very little knowledge I had he looked like the perfect dog. He was friendly and loved a fuss. I cannot explain how big his head looked but he was a Rotti with a lovely big head and very mastiff features. According to my new boss he was trainable and easy to get on with.

When I first got him I took a drive straight to a pet shop because I had some supplies but didn't account for his sheer bulk when I had bought his bowls and bed. He was 50kg of lean Rotti, stunning looks and stubborn as a mule.

As time went on I came to know he was not just dog aggressive but anything furry aggressive, cats, squirrels anything. But not people, never people.

I had a kennel delivered and built on the same day I picked him up. He had no problem with getting in the kennel as he was used to living in one, he couldn't live in the house because we had a Cocker Spaniel and a Persian cat. Not to mention the fact he had weed up the telly on our first attempt to allow him access to the house.

I took him to work the first night, when I turned up it really hit me that I had no idea what I was doing or what I was meant to do.

With George's new collar and lead I took him out of the car and followed the dog handler on site around while he gave me the guided tour and gossip. I swapped with him and he gave me my radio and the low down on what I was to do.

I guess I hoped that a 6'2" bloke and a 50kg Rotti would put most people off. But then I found out who I was looking after and realised it wouldn't and actually, not much would.

I was working alongside Special Forces guys and what I would class as the real deal in Close Protection, trying my hardest to wing it.

I remember walking past people telling them not to come to close to George because of his propensity to violence, hoping they wouldn't notice his stump wagging for a stroke.

These were my beginnings; I really didn't have a clue what I was letting myself in for.

Long 12 hour nights with the possibility of no staff turning up the next day and my shift turning into 24 or even 36 hours, sat in a cramped Volvo estate at the end of someone's garden. Hoping I wouldn't get wet, because if you got wet at the beginning of your shift you stayed wet until you got home. I discovered a cold and wet that I had never experienced before, a cold that the heaters in the car couldn't shake off. It was horrendous and by the time I got home I was regularly freezing cold and bone tired. A tiredness again that I had never encountered, after walking around site through all of the unnatural hours trying to remain alert and trying my very hardest to find new methods of staying awake which became more and more difficult the more shifts you did and the more bored you got. I used to read a lot but straining your eyes for hours was more likely to put me to sleep but you couldn't sit and do nothing and as much as I tried to concentrate on dog training it was impossible to train George for 12 hours.

This is dog handling, it wasn't the glamour I had expected, I worked for some amazingly well known and well connected people, but conditions never really got better.

You were always just the bloke sat on someone's drive in your van or car patrolling a dog round somebody's property so the burglars would go next door rather than try it on with your dog.

I learnt a lot in that first 6 months, a lot on how to keep comfortable, warm and how to stay up for the whole night when nothing was happening and how to keep on the move when the Boss was in residence. When the boss was in we had to patrol regularly, 15 minutes in 15 minutes patrolling. That was hard work, luckily the boss didn't hang around too much, and the house was his sanctuary when he wanted to get away from it all. He had other houses around and over time I got to know the handlers on some of the other sites.

After 6 months I was starting to lose my passion for it, this wasn't what I signed up for. Every week I would have to fight my boss for my wages and every day, usually 7 days a week I would walk around a property that was beautiful but even beauty can become quite mundane after a while.

I wasn't getting any help with training and although I was reading books and trying to glean some knowledge from them I wasn't really getting anywhere. George had bitten my cat in half and wasn't particularly popular at home. That's a true story.

Something needed to change; unfortunately all of the people I changed over with were not too good at Dog Handling either. Most saw it as a way of getting some sleep at night while they were supposed to be working or had their vans or cars converted so it was like camping with TVs and cookers it was like home away from home. But none trained their dogs and my motivation to get my George to the top of his game and what I had seen on You Tube and envisioned me doing with him was getting further and further away.

I worked there in total for about three years, with other jobs and events in-between times. It was the beginning for me and gave me a great insight into the world. It was either hard graft or nothing was happening, there was no middle ground. But in all of this I got to spend every evening playing with my dog. I became known to a few connected people and got some great work with really famous people. It was like a dream.

As long as I had something to keep me occupied I could stay awake and I enjoyed training George although it was sometimes frustrating beyond words. There was a large adventure playground that was deserted and I was given permission to allow George to run around it.

I had never seen George so happy as when he was running around playing all over the obstacles and it was big enough for him to get quite a speed up. I could close us in which meant it was the only time he could run free due to his dog aggression. They were some beautiful evenings and though the site was small compared to the ones I would work later in my career George and I had great fun. It was when he was his happiest and he was such an affectionate character that I used to chat to regularly and implore him to do as he was told in our training sessions but he rarely listened.

He was a happy, fun loving dog and he was great to work with and I could forgive his stubbornness easily because I put it down to my training, I had very little knowledge and was just happy with my new job and my new friend however wet and cold it got.

By chance I was talking to a guy who also worked for my boss and had come to take over from me, he said he knew of a trainer who ran a club of dog handlers on a Thursday, everyone met up and spent the day training for agility, obedience and bite work. I was given this gentleman's number and told to ring him. We will call him M, to enhance his mystery and so he can't sue me. Not that I think he would, just in case he wants to sue me for that.

The handsome, happy meathead that was George.

That day I rang the number I had been given. He was great to have a chat with and it sounded like it was just a group of like-minded people getting together in a field that he hired and running through some training methods.

M said I could come along and have a look. But to come regularly was at his discretion, he did all the training hired the field so of course that was fine.

I was so excited, this could be it. Training meant I could get George right, I had seen videos on social media of dogs doing amazing things and I thought if I could just get the idea and flow of training I could adapt to get George really spot on. I was having no joy with him as it was and apart from a few simple commands and heel work I hadn't really progressed at all.

This would mean the world to me as I could class myself as a proper Dog Handler not just playing at it and trying out random people's suggestions that I met up with. If I could just learn how to do a few bits I then had plenty of time to polish up on his training. This may be exactly the break I needed the training was in Newbury in a field and M supplied coffee and lunch in the form of a BBQ.

The day came and I made my way to Newbury.

I remember turning into the field seeing all these smart vans, tailgates open and built in cages with dogs just laid out enjoying the fresh air.

People in black uniforms wandering around getting water for their dogs and maybe stretching their legs. I felt a bit at a loss because I had none of this kit, I didn't even know where to get it. I had leads and collars from pet shops a van that though was fit for purpose was nowhere near as smart as all of these others. I had a cage from a pet shop that I had used bent over nails to secure onto the ply lining in the van I had bought, next to their custom built setups with draws for their dog toys, bowls and equipment. I was feeling like the poor cousin.

The one thing that really struck me was how different these people were to the people I had worked with so far. They had all the equipment; the dogs were under control, well groomed. My heart jumped. If only I could learn from this lot.

I parked up and a guy that I came to know as M walked over and introduced himself.

We had a good chat about what I knew and what I had done.

I explained how green I was and that I really needed to learn. I'm sure I came across as humble and a bit ignorant because I knew next to nothing about this. This was the moment I made up my mind that this was where I needed to be to learn. M said *"can I have a look in your van, you can train with us but I need to know you take this seriously."*

Then came a barrage of questions about my equipment, nothing about my dog. *"Do you have a first aid kit?"* I'm sure I looked stumped but reached into the van and got my first aid kit to show him. *"And for the dog?"* It just so happened I did. I took that out and he opened it up and inspected it. *"Needs some more bits in there but good."*

"Now let's have a look at your dog and your collars and leads."

This said so much to me, this was what I needed. Somebody to show me the ways from the ground up. Dog Handling is as much about getting the right equipment and feeding your dog the right food as it is training. It is so important to be comfortable and as dry as possible to make the job more palatable to make sure your dog is eating well so he is as healthy as possible and his coat is as protective as it can be. All this is just as important it greases the wheels.

I got George and M commented on the size of his head, everyone did. He had a huge head.

"Do you have spare collars and leads?" *"No"* so M listed a few things I needed to get but seemed happy with what I had for now. "You can do the training with us and if you do well, you can come back regularly"

I did continue to go, the information I gleaned from the professional members and watching the training gave me great ideas.

The main thing when you are learning from other people is, even if you're learning what you won't be doing with your dog, you are still learning.

I had a great time; this is where I first met Phil Nash. A big guy from Birmingham who had a lot of knowledge about dogs and the industry and said it how it was.

We instantly got on and paired up as the dynamic duo. Whenever there was mischief to get up to it was usually Phil or his brother.

Phil and I used training to have a giggle. Usually we had both worked the night before and were most probably working that evening as well. So we used to put our dogs through their paces but more than anything our sarcasm and immature humour would get a run out. He kept me sane on the days when you struggled to go training through tiredness or my guilt at constantly not being at home. We would muck about, take the mick out of other dogs and dog handlers, purely light hearted banter. Usually the giggles we had were at other people's expense but never malicious.

Phil and I remain good friends although he will deny that. If I wanted to ring someone that would insult me within thirty seconds of answering, it would be him.

We remind ourselves of it all reasonably regularly. When a friend of ours forgot to turn his tyre pump off and it exploded his tyre. Most of us dropped to the ground wondering what the hell had happened. The chances of shots fired in rural Berkshire were slim but the fear gave way to hysterical laughter.

There was one guy who had a lovely little Mali, we used to tease him quite a lot because his dog was small.

We used social media to put pictures of fruit bats, foxes, and all sorts on his account. It was a giggle and we all suffered a lot of banter. For me it was always about George's agility or dog aggression. George wasn't built for agility and looked like a Sloth compared to the 20kg Mali's whipping over jumps and dog walks Followed by George who had a habit of just putting his head down and crashing through things.

Phil even got blamed for causing a bite once when this ladies Rotti bit her on the knee. It wasn't an epic bite more of a protest but Phil and I were a good 50 metres away having a chat. Phil ran over with the first aid kit from his van. It was unusual enough to see him run but to run to help someone else was unheard of. As he approached she started shouting at him, blaming him for winding her dog up.

41

I think it because most things that were pranks or if someone was to be blamed it was usually Phil or I.

We would run our dogs over the agility course and though George couldn't do obedience near the other dogs we used to do it a little way away, I felt sort of included. I mean I could still hear everyone else. The idea was to desensitise him to the other dogs presence. In time I hoped this would work and I would be able to get closer and closer until eventually there would be a day when I could join in with everyone else. That was the idea, the practice was very different. From this account it all sounds very serene, it wasn't. Such was the strength of George and his intensity around other dogs I felt like I was holding back a cart horse, he would bounce up and down to get to the other dogs, earning him the nickname of "Tigger". It wasn't serene or pleasant.

Then we would go to work that night, ring Phil and put the world to rights on the phone. I think the phone networks breathed a sigh of relief when we weren't on shift together. I won't name all of the people I met Dog Handling, some I know won't care, some won't like what I say. So apart from a select few I won't name associates.

I met some amazing people and some that defied belief as in most professions. Hence the separation of Dog Handlers and dog handlers.

This was the real beginning of my Dog Handling, although there will be people reading this book who will disagree with M's training. One thing I learnt really quickly about Dog Handlers and trainers. The only thing two of them will agree on is that the third one is doing it wrong.

There is so much turmoil in the dog world over methods and personalities, ethics and standards that you have to just stay out of it and take the teachings where you can without burning any bridges.

This isn't easy, as in many things in life now there are forums where people who have never met, who have never seen each other's dogs perform or their work ethics argue and bitch over exactly that. It's incredible.

I was thrown off a couple of these sites because playing devil's advocate is my default setting.

I remember having a heated debate with a few people about electronic collars. Though I completely understand the revulsion that people feel over this, it's an emotive subject.

But I was trying to explain that if used properly and if used as a last resort I would use one, if all other techniques had been exhausted and it would have to be over something really important. The example I was trying to cite was a guy had a dog that chased car wheels, but only while they were moving. He had tried all sorts of techniques and nothing was working. He lived on a field so this little dog would chase the tractors, the quads, anything. So they used an electronic collar. Not as a means of punishment but on its lowest setting it was like clicking your fingers. Just enough to grab the dog's attention.

What I was trying to get across was faced with imminent death under a set of wheels or an electronic collar and life; I would choose the electronic collar as long as it was used properly.

This was enough to get me kicked off the forum.

M's training, ignited my passion in training dogs and showed me that out there in the dog world were people trying to do it right, not just sleeping at night and having teeth on the end of a lead or dogs too lazy or insecure to protect themselves or their handler.

They gave me something to aspire too. These people had passion, a competitive streak and a goal to achieve.

These thoughts were compounded when I saw a few of the regulars at M's run their dogs over the agility or do some bite work.

The control some of these guys had and the way their dogs went in for bites or over obstacles were amazing. I can't explain, this was like the Holy Grail to me, man and dog working together as a pack, protecting each other.

One of the very first dogs I saw going over this was a little Mali called George, he was so fast and obedient and though the power in the bite was lacking and he definitely wasn't a manstopper. His accuracy, speed and control were incredible. The speed at which he attacked with gave him more oomph but he was only about 20kgs so he needed to put all of his speed into it. But 10/10 for everything else. He was told to go in, he went in, and out he came out straight away. It was something to behold.

I don't know where the quote comes from but someone said to me once "the way to wind up a dog handler is to attack the dog and the way to wind up the dog is attack the handler" this was the bond most of these guys had.

They had a respect and relationship with their dogs that far outweighed what I had seen so far. It was the boost I needed and I grabbed it with both hands.

They were all at varying levels of training but they were all head and shoulders above George and me.

This was George not long after I got him. He was a beautiful powerful dog with a stubborn streak a mile wide.

While I was chatting to some of the regular guys reality struck. Nobody scoffed at my lack of knowledge and I was very much welcomed. But in the back of my mind was always the thought that I would need a different dog to George if I was going to rival these guys.

M set up a mock exercise that involved M hiding in a copse behind some trees. The dog and handler entered the copse and the dog was to find and indicate towards M, if the dog didn't indicate M would move around making rustling noises. When the dog indicated M would come forward shouting depending on the robustness of the dog. If the dog was trained to bite and release M would take a bite. I later found out this was a search and indication. Followed by a controlled bite and a release when commanded. A few of the regulars went ahead and did the exercise with varying degrees of success.

Different suggestions were made to enhance the dogs and their abilities which were all to be worked on but all of them protected the handler well. I was very impressed. M instructed me to get George out and came with me to show me the protocol to keep everyone safe, these dogs were keyed up and ready to go so best to be cautious.

When you got to the back of the vehicle, you were to look all around and shout "*dog out.*" When confident nobody was about you could let the dog out. Something else I needed to work on. As you opened his cage door he would try and barge past me to get out. Watching everyone else their dogs would sit and wait for them to clip the lead on.

George however wasn't keyed up or ready to go. In fact he wasn't interested in the slightest. He came out, stretched and looked around for the first thing to pee up.

His interest was only peaked when he noticed other dogs; he nearly pulled my arm out of its socket trying to get to them. It was horrific. I could do nothing with him, he barked and pulled and growled.

The power that he had in his body and the way he could use it to move left to right and front and back would leave me trying to hold on to him a bit like Marlin fishing except I think George had more energy just based on his obsession and intensity. It was horrible to watch and hear. The sound coming from his mouth was like a low grumble it was so menacing, he would bounce up and down and nothing else mattered in those moments. Complete focus on the dog or dogs. I would try and calm him down but if you touched he would swing his head round to you at such speed there was a fear he would bite and though he never did, the speed at which he moved and the grumbling was enough to put me off testing it again.

For the next six months this was the agenda. Week in week out I went and every time he just wanted to kill every dog he saw, we didn't improve at all really. His only focus was the other dogs, so much so that he had no room for anything but that.

Every week I used to clear up the excrement from the back of the van when he got so aggressive and stressed about the other dogs being there, he would get diarrhoea. It was horrific not just because of the obvious smell, noise and frustration but I could only guess at what was going through his mind and the stress he must be going through. The whole time I was kidding myself that this would help and one day like a dam breaking there would be an outpouring of love or an epiphany where George would suddenly get it and give up on his persecution of other dogs.

Me and him continued to work every night and continued to train but we were getting nowhere. I was learning loads from the other dogs but nothing from George except my shoulder was beginning to resemble that of an English archer from holding on to him every week.

Nothing was ever going to come of George in this arena, he was too dog aggressive and I couldn't get him to focus, he was great at work and a lovely dog to be around but the time came when I realised I would never be able to rehabilitate him.

I called the kennel I got him from and they were happy to have him back and were very apologetic that they hadn't explained further about his dog aggression. I was gutted, I dropped him off one day and the drive back was emotional. I had never felt such a feeling of loss. It's hard with dogs because as I explore later on there is nothing you can say to reassure them and nothing they can say to take away any of the guilt or pain. With a person, most people you could have a rational chat and make them understand but with dogs they are completely dependent on you and you're decisions alone more to the point we don't know if that decision is right or wrong. The confusion in his eyes as I walked away brought a painful lump to my throat trying to hold back my emotions. As much as George was hard work around dogs on his own he was great and he had become a good friend from sitting in the van all night I had learnt all his little idiosyncrasies. I had watched him run around the play park at work and really enjoy himself. I had taken him on some lovely walks just me and him out in the back of beyond always because I couldn't be anywhere around other animals. I realised then I knew little about his history. I didn't even know his age.

Part of me was frustrated with myself. I just couldn't get him to work; I couldn't even get him to listen when another dog was in the mix. If I could have done he would have been perfect. There are many in the dog handling world who don't believe Rottweiler's have what it takes. I would have loved to have proved them wrong because Rotti's are an awesome dog in so many ways. Loyal, powerful and if you ever wanted a deterrent they are it. I remember having this conversation many times with friends. You have different dogs which are generally used, GSD, Rotti's and Belgian Shepherds.

Each has their speciality as I will go into later, but if you want people to leave your site, or an area. Get a Rotti out and very few will stand their ground. Films and the media have maligned this dog to a point where the perception helped me do my job.

It is also sad because treated right they are such a lovely and loving dog. Loyal to the end, funny and full of character. On a downside they are not for the inexperienced or feint hearted.

The problem was, George hadn't been brought up right and this impaired many things. First and foremost it was stressing him out so much trying to be a protection dog and trying to change his temperament that it really wasn't fair on him.

Secondly if he saw a dog while we were working, there was no calming him down.

Thirdly, he wouldn't protect me, and if he did he had no training in what that looked like so if he did protect me I couldn't be sure where he would bite, what he would bite and if he would let go when told.

It was a complete failure and I took it very personally.

After spending my life believing dogs were my thing and I had a way with them I had to accept that some dogs just couldn't be helped because of past experience, lack of socialisation. Whatever it was it put me back in my confidence a lot and left George back in a kennel which was the last thing I ever wanted.

I was now doing bits of work all over, my boss had decided because I was smart, turned up and stayed awake all night I was a cut above the rest.

The bar wasn't set very high in his world. But I ended up plodding around, still working for the Russian but I was lucky enough to get night shifts on traveller sites, famous peoples estates, and on business estate that I became quite fond off.

The problem always was George, I didn't have any confidence so after knowing a guy I worked with was moving off into another area of expertise he was looking to rehome his dog.

I had said to him from the time I met Max that I would take him if he was ever to need to rehome him.

The time came when Carl decided to go back to being a magician. Yes a magician

Max was a beautiful gold sable GSD. Weighing in at about 34kg he was lot smaller than George but really athletic. He was an ex prison dog allegedly and well trained, he would bark up on command. I was told he could bite and release on command along with all sorts of other commands of which I probably never found out.

I went to Hemel Hemptstead to pick him up a couple of days after taking George back to the kennel.

Getting Max felt like a new beginning. He was a great looking GSD gold sable and had a beautifully proud stand. He was always up straight and alert. It seemed like he was always on full alert. He was slim and deep chested with an intensity in his eyes that never seemed to recede. He was attentive and his default position was stood right next to me and always looked ready to go.

The funniest thing was, it was not only his physical presence that was different from George. Max never seemed to sleep or slow down. He never really looked at the floor. He was always head up chest out and storming along, his head would switch left to right constantly. He was so watchful and his energy was like a childs on skittles.

Max looked to me and the bond I felt pretty much straight away. What I was to learn about Max was that it was nothing to do with bond. He had worked and trained from a young age in the prisons. He was more than likely multi handled which meant he was just taken from the kennels by whoever was going to work him that shift.He bonded temporarily with whoever held the lead.I didn't know this at the beginning and took all the credit for such a swift bond.

Training, patrolling, working, chasing tennis balls. All other times he seemed miserable, but as soon as the uniform was on and he was in the cage his ears went up, he was constantly alert. You could walk a site 3mx3m all night and he would be as interested on his 20th patrol as he was on his first.

This was the beauty of GSD's which in my small experience does out rank Rotti's. Rotti's basically fall asleep on the second patrol. They have a short attention span. If there is trouble or a disturbance they are back on it. Always up for a fight but GSD's are constantly attentive from the first patrol to last. This is a generalisation he says as he hears all the Rotti owners slamming the book shut.

This may sound crazy but dog owners, whether they are working them or not have their favourites just like car owners. But I have found owners of working breeds such as GSD owners and Rotti owners are some of the most ardent. Again a generalisation before I upset all other dog owners.

He was the perfect working dog, at home he wasn't lively or fun but he was well behaved and great with the kids and our pets. You could take him for a lovely long walk and he would get on with all the other dogs and people.

Some of my interest in dog handling was it allowed me to own a dog of my choice, I've always been a sucker for a big dog and with a normal job I couldn't because of work and exercising him. With dog handling I could do all of this, one of my favourite past times was walking with Max, I couldn't do it with George, but with Max you could let him off and he would run around and enjoy his walk and I could take in all of the nature and the forests in our local area. It was a real joy, if you're a nature lover or dog walker yourselves you'll know what I mean.

My children fell in love with him and he tolerated them.

My friend Ben took the preceding picture of Max, he took several on that day. I would throw the ball and Ben would sit with his camera as Max shot past and adjust his shutter speed everytime. We looked through the photo's and it was picture after picture of the end of Max's tail. He was so quick and never tired.

The picture was taken at Swinley Forest in Bracknell and we were so lucky to get some amazing shots of Max.
He was a truly stunning dog.

Trust in me my friend for I am your comrade.
I will protect you with my last breath.
When all others have left you and the loneliness of the night closes in,
I will be at your side.

The main reason for moving George on was my safety and his happiness, as the sites and jobs came rolling in I was asked to do more and more riskier sites, the business estate I mentioned was a bit of a hotspot for trouble and my lack of trust in George and wether he would protect me it starts impacting on your confidence to deal with some situations.

So the relief when I first took Max to work and a friend of mine Keith Davies agreed to take a bite. Max was a average size GSD, 34kgs but he was so rapid across the ground.

Keith agreed to bait Max when we were at work one night. I wanted to know if Max would protect and part of working dogs is to know how your dog works. Will he go in on command, does he need to be wound up. What gets him going, it can go from whispering to ignite their suspicion to full on shouting to agitate the dog and then just point and launch. It all depends on the dog especially if thy have already been trained. Carl had given me som tips, an instruction manual if you will but I needed to know if this would work the same for me with commands and little idiosyncrasies. It is so important for the handler to really get to know his dog because there may be little things that the handler will need to compensate for or cover so the baiter/criminal doesn't get to see.

We had decided we would go for a passive bite for the sake of Max, he didn't know me yet so to ask him to protect me under pressure would be unfair. A passive bite lacked pressure. It is a bite done purely by command, the baiter stays inanimate and even turns sideways to be as unthreatening as possible. This is a test on two levels. It tests if Max will work purely on command. Imagine someone walks up to you calmly with a knife in his hand. He could be threatening you and your dog but with no raised voices your dog might not pick up on the cues so it is always important to know your dog will attack with vigour just on command. Also it tested him on the quality of his bite.There was no pressure or movement so your dog could place his bite where he wanted to, you get to see where he wants to. Keith got ready, sleeve on, no pressure or anger just a passive bite.

I walked up close to Keith, control is essential. Max knew what was coming. His ears flicked forward and his chest puffed out. His legs suddenly became stiff and he seemed to grow an inch or two in height as he approached. In the moment of heightened focus they become quick in their ovements. I guess it could be confused with twitchiness but it is more like they look back to you but have to

50

quickly snap back to watch the man in front. The best analogy is when you are driving and joining a busy motorway from the slip road. But instead of other cars the dog is looking for your approval or your cue to do what they are trained to do.

The puffing up and posturing is all bravado that I was to learn confident dogs did. It was like a boxer getting in the ring daring his opponent to fight and making himself as big as he could be. The only difference for dogs is that the plan is to scare or intimidate the challenger so they don't have to fight. To fight is counter productive as I will cover later they may get hurt and that isn't good for them or the pack. So they intimidate first and hope you back down.

Max was on the end of the lead, not pulling just keeping it taught, like he wanted to feel the pressure and know I was there. This way he could feel the give when I let go. Many dogs will do this, they feel there way as you move forward they move. The last thing you want is a dog on a slack lead not knowing what you are up to. You are a team. Part of that team can easily go rogue given the room to.

He surprised me when I thought his bark would come but he kept his mouth quite closed and then as we got closer he started grumbling. This was all to become clear to me the whys and wherefore of his behaviour as I learnt from him.

As we got to within range he started barking, a deep but sharp bark, it had urgency to it. A sharpness and a depth that I hadn't heard. I knew then instinctively he was up for this.His front feet raised as he pulled against his collar he strained to make those couple of inches closer to his prey. The whole time I was whispering to him, implying urgency and suspicion to him like an earworm. His jowls were raised and his teeth on show there was a frantic side to him, he had lost his cool, calm demeanour for now and the spit was flying from his mouth, teeth on show. I was expecting to see the whites of his eyes to add to the madness that he exuded but his eyes were like millponds, completely still, one focus and focused they were. I didn't realise fully until then how much effort they put into intimidating their opponent. Max looked like a lunatic but his eyes showed he was completely in control and that was scarier.

Keith moved his arm, a signal to tell me he was ready. I shouted "hold him" assertively and Max flew, no run up, but the take off was incredible the bite was inch perfect. His mouth struck the sleeve with power and speed and the bite was right in the middle. I hadn't handled a dog who bit on command, the adrenalin that coursed through was a feeling I had never had before.

It was great, I'm not a macho man but my god I enjoyed that, so much so I was enthralled watching Max. Keith was going with the fight as we had discussed, Max was fighting hard to suppress Keith and show him who was boss when I had

51

seen enough I called "out" Keith became motionless and Max instantly dropped off the sleeve into a posture ready to go again.

His teeth were out and he only had eyes for Keith. Keith was much more experienced with dogs than I and he said "*go again*". I didn't need convincing, I said the word and in he went again. No fear, no second thoughts. Just straight in, the sleeve right to the back of the mouth which I had learnt was the best result you could get from a dog and meant confidence.

I was so happy. I told him to "*out*" and ran off stroking him and telling him what a great lad he was. Keith gave him a wide berth and came over. "*That was great*" he said. "*at least you know he'll do it*".

I couldn't wipe the smile off my face. For the first time I felt I might actually become a respected Dog Handler and be able to learn so much from Max.I put him in his cage and we went in to have a cuppa in our portacabin.

As we sat and chewed the fat about how impressive Max had been and how we could test him and try different things, the whole time I was in a state of nirvana.

It is difficult to explain how hard the decision to say goodbye to George was and how if Max hadn't worked it would have compounded the grief I felt and the feeling of incompetence. These are all selfish emotions but knowing George was somewhere safe and clean and he was loved there I was allowed to ponder these emotions with a clean conscience.

As I said earlier, my affinity with dogs is very strong and unfortunately with this comes a huge sense of sadness when any animal is treated badly or goes through misfortune because they are such a pure animal. They don't deserve any sadness or pain, karma should not apply to dogs because when have they never knowingly done anything out of malice to anyone or anything else? I digress!!

The point is with Max being the perfect dog at home, at the park, with family and other pets it made me feel more comfortable about handing George back, knowing I now had a dog that would protect me. We used to have great fun at the park and I cannot explain how this is the joy of dog ownership for me. After a long night at work I could take Max to the park or to the forest and let him run what was left of his energy playing with the other dogs. He would always run ahead of the rest and they would happily follow or chase dependant on perspective. It was lovely and started a habit that I have to this day. After a stressful day the first thing I do is put Hooch's collar on and go and while away an hour or two in the fresh air just me and he.

He wouldn't just protect me, he was trained to work for anyone, there was some loyalty but a lot of it was a protective streak born of his training. He was such a great dog, he was very much like a robot. There was little feeling for anything but working, training and playing ball.

He was also immaculately well behaved and would walk beautifully to heel. He wouldn't react to other dogs while he was at work At home he would sleep and the kids could sleep with their heads on his chest and he wouldn't bother. He gave the air of contentment although I swear it was boredom at home.

I carried on with Max for over a year, I didn't train him. He trained me, every time I met someone new it seemed they would tell me something about their dog and I would try it on Max and he would respond. Max taught me, for over a year I learnt all the things a dog could teach me. All the things a dog could do. It was incredible and he was incredible.

I was still working at a Business estate in Reading at the time and coming into contact with many new Dog Handlers and I really felt safe with Max, we had a lot to deal with. Drug dealers finding somewhere quiet to do their deals, ladies of the night looking for the same, kids in their cars finding somewhere to do burnouts and play silly games in their cars. It was busy, but with a dog that would do whatever you asked it was great. I even had the chance of working him during a protest that came about on site. Max never missed a beat, with the noise and bustle and all the people he remained calm and just did what I asked him to do with a level head. It was my first and last protest. We had been made aware in the morning that there may be a protest against one of the business's on the park and for obvious reasons the park management wanted it to stay as peaceful and contained as possible for the sake of the other tenants. So by lunchtime on came a group of several hundred people banging drums and pots and pans. It was quite intimidating but also the rush you get from it is like nothing I'd ever felt before. I felt excited and apprehensive all in one. We waited by the company premises for the demonstrators, although it was a peaceful demo it had to be contained and kept safe. It is difficult to keep things calm, if your dog is barking up and showing teeth you tend to find it raises the tempo of the confrontation and it can escalate very quickly. This is the beauty of Max, he was nice and calm and didn't seem threatened by anything. He calmly wandered next to me adhering to commands I gave him. It all went very well and apart from having to herd a few trouble makers there were no problems. Partly due to Max's calmness and my confidence in his ability to deal with whatever came up. Confidence in your dog makes a huge difference to how you approach situations.

I remember the day I was walking Max and he seemed to have developed a limp, I took it easy on him for a few days but the limp wasn't going away.

I took him to hydrotherapy at a place called Aqua doggies, they were great. Max loved it once he got into it, and Max wasn't one to tire easy but swimming really took it out of him. But the great thing is it puts no pressure on their limbs and joints. We had a few sessions and it didn't help, Max enjoyed it but it had no bearing on his limp. So I took the decision to go to the vets.

He had x-Ray's and tests but nothing seemed to come of it. The vet didn't know what it was, only that it was getting worse. No matter how easy I took it on him.

Some nights I would rest him completely doing all the patrols in the van but still the limp was seemingly beginning to hurt him a lot. The amount of walking we had to do at work sometimes was just compounding the problem, the times he had to rear up and threaten people on site was an all to common problem and all of it was putting pressure on his back leg.

Then it really hit home one night when I finished work and he couldn't put his foot down at all. He was on three legs and stayed on three legs for several days after.

I took some time off and had him rest his leg, he was caged mostly for this time to see if resting it would help, my friend Phil Nash used to tease me, saying I had broken my dog. Too much walking because in my shifts I rarely rested. I used to give the dog time to recover but we were a very active team. Mainly because it was the only way I could stay awake on the long and sometimes boring nights.

Also it was for the dog, when you work dogs you get a lot of criticism from people that may be ignorant or have their view and stick to it. Working dogs have great lives if treated right. Loads of exercise, stimulation. Good diet and the best healthcare because by default you don't want them to be ill or slothenly.

A working dog rarely stops training and by default if the training is done properly it is all fun. Trust me, working dogs are not to be pitied. Hooch looked and acted like a puppy until he was into double figures purely because of a good diet, exercise, stimulation and a few cuddles.

I took Max back to the vets and to my surprise the vet had come up with a possible diagnosis.

Contracture of the Gracilis. This was a rare complaint and the way it was described to me was, if I imagined an elastic band, tied it in a knot, and then another knot and slowly the band would lose its elasticity. This was what was happening to Maxs muscle in his back leg. As his muscle got tired it got tighter and lifted it off the ground.

There was no cure and taking his leg off, him being a big dog would come with its own problems. He could live a normal life but his activity would have to come right down to next to nothing. Work was out of the question.

I talk about it calmly now, but at the time I was so guilty, upset annoyed. Apparently this kind of complaint comes from a possible trauma to that muscle earlier in life. I don't know, and as he was a rehomed dog per say, I knew little of his former life.

The main thing was, he had to be rehomed. Another dog, but this time it was a dog I had really come to depend on, he was a great partner. Not really my mate, but a great partner. Like the sort of person you would employ or go to work with because they could do the job, but wouldn't necessarily go for a beer with after work.

Again there was that guilt, I thought seriously about giving up Dog Handling at this point. I just didn't seem to do well with them. I started blaming my self for all the exercise and work I did. But this was what dogs do. I couldn't get to grips with it. Had I worked him into the ground. I mean, when I say we were active I don't mean hundreds of miles I just mean we used to walk a bit. Nothing compared to what a dog is capable of.

It hit me hard and the guilt of how it would affect Max was killing me.

So he was taken by my wife to a rehoming centre that we knew off and the lady knew a lady who wanted a GSD male to go with her ageing female and look after their property. But live indoors as a pet. Nice bit of land, could do as much or as little as his leg permitted and would be loved.

Again I find it so hard to explain, but I'm sure the dog lovers out there will absolutely understand. I let another dog down.

There are dog handlers out there or owners of working dogs in general who treat their dogs like a tool. Not badly but they matter little to them but a means to an end. I had met a few of these and like I say, they don't mistreat the dog but they have little emotion for them and when the dog is done they just move them on.

I could never be like this. I had and probably always will have a love for them and all of my dogs have had a place in my heart that is akin to family. I'm certainly not ashamed of it, no animal deserves poor treatment. Except maybe wasps.

In my mind I did and still do truly believe that a working dog treated right is a happy dog. Dogs were built, bred, evolved to do this. All the training you do with them is only honing their natural instincts to protect, to hunt, to scent and track. Its all natural and hence i believe it to be good for them.

Max was the second dog I could not keep as a working dog. I was gutted and due to the nature of the business and other dogs I couldn't keep him as a pet either. We had a Cocker Spaniel called Daisy which was my wifes, a cat, and with Max, where was I going to put another working dog?

So it had to be and I was gutted, I felt like I had done him wrong. It took me a while to get over it and made worse by a revelation a year or so later. I will digress to explain the story because if I put it in later, you will probably have forgotten.

I went to training with Mick, I was chatting to him one day on a break from training Polar about Max and his problem. I was stunned when my trainer said, "I had a dog with that" I looked at him aghast and said, "what did you do, I rehomed my boy." Mick looked at me like I was mad, "My boy worked and trained until he was 11, you know you can just have that muscle snipped, then they rely on the other muscles."

Apparently Mick knew of a dog physio that specialised in racing dogs and this was a reasonably common occurence. I have no evidence of how common it is but Mick said it is perfectly treatable and leaves the dog with very little in the way of after effects.

This was possibly the worst news I could have heard. Max was great and if this was true I probably could have worked with Mr Dependable for many years after with no problem although this would have changed my journey. I was now gutted and angry, but a good year or more on there was nothing to be done but change vet and store the info.

Together we will conquer all obstacles,
and search out those who might wish harm to others.
All I ask of you is compassion, the caring touch of your hands.
It is for you that I will unselfishly give my life and spend nights unrested.
Although our days together may be marked by the passing of the seasons.
Know that each day at your side is my reward.

After Max had gone I had very little fire in my belly for training.

I used to go training, I don't know why I didn't have a dog. I used to borrow Keiths dog for work so I could carry on working but it's never the same.

The confidence you feel in the bond and the knowledge of their capability is comforting and gives you reassurance. Even down to the silly little things they do that give you confidence in their familiarity is all gone. You have no bond or wish to bond because they have to go back to their owners eventually.

It was a difficult time, the feelings of guilt have never really left me but at that time they were so strong. I was toying with the idea of getting a proper job and just coming out of it. I genuinely thought I would never find another dog that was so uncomplicated and so well trained as Max and the feeling I had let him down was making me doubt my ability and my ability to bond with another dog.

I carried on going training for the fun of it and the comradery. But like I say my passion had ebbed. Watching all the other people with their dogs was enjoyable but also was a bit painful and the joy and fun of the last couple of years felt like it might just have to be a memory as I didn't feel I had the heart for this anymore. Both were difficult decisions and more than that I felt like someone somewhere was trying to make me understand that it was time to look for a different direction. Dog Handling had done what I needed it to do and as a family we were financially stable and my wife was able to go back to work if necessary. While waiting for a better idea I continued as I was with Keiths dog.

While I was at training M approached me, said he had a dog that was in need of rehoming. He explained he was a bit of a mess cosmetically as he had been handed around and nobody could really get on with him. He wasn't aggressive just insular and shied away from people.

I asked to have a look and M got him out of his van.

He was a big white GSD, he was matted and feeling sorry for himself. His body language said he was done and fed up but there was a fire behind his eyes that told me everything I needed to know.

I took the lead and he instantly looked up at me and I knew he was for me. I walked of with him and he heeled next to me nicely. He walked so close his matted coat rubbed against my leg. At intervals he would look up at me and his eyes were pleading to me to take him. I knew I would.

I don't know if it is in a dogs makeup to manipulate the owner to show a bond that isn't there or if they choose who they want and are honest in their appealing looks and if I'm honest I don't care. It felt like Polar picked me and similar to all the dogs I have had from the first couple of minutes I knew I was taking them home.I feel blessed with the dogs I've had but I don't know if it's been their choice or mine.

Polar was no different, his imploring eyes and neglected looks made my mind up and yes I am a soft touch. I am also very self aware so I know I am a soft touch. This doesn't change the fact that I am a soft touch.

I fell in love with him and I think the feeling was mutual. What a great boy.

He was a mixture of George and Max. He was quite thick set which was accentuated by his unkempt coat. He had a wide muzzle, wider than your average GSD and definitely wider than Max's. But a powerful build under that coat and slightly underweight but he seemed in good health other than that. His coat needed work but as soon s he was settled and eating properly it always amazes me how quickly animals can recover.

He was slightly nervous but knew what he had to do. He only had eyes for me but his nervousness had resulted in a few issues.

I walked him around the training ground and as we got to know each other he started trotting like a palameno. It was a beautiful thing to watch him as he transformed and his nervousness with me dissipated. I brought the tempo up and he started aligning himself with me.

His tempo took a couple of seconds but he came up and down to match what I was doing. I tried a few simple commands and he followed nicely.

Its lovely when you walk a dog and you get that feeling. Its a feeling of comradery I guess. A feeling that someone or something in this world is aligning itself to you instead of the other way around. An animal that understands nothing of what you say but everything that you mean. I guess it is like many things in life, people go to see puppies and know exactly the one they want or get a feeling from a house they are viewing. It is instinctive more than anything and like these things I couldn't explain what it was but something drew me to Poley and it wasn't his name which I tried to change but couldnt't.

All the things running through my head, how I was going to train him, how I would start. How I would explain to my wife at the time that I had bought a dog.

I told M I would have him and if I could I would take him today.

Many people took the mick about how brave I was working a pretty white dog. But I didn't care. He was such a good fit. Within quarter of an hour we had an understanding.

M said he had been picked up as a stray and nobody really had much more history than that on him.It just made me want him more and give him a good life and show him how life could be for a dog. A working dog.

I took him home and introduced him to the family. He had a little habit of grumbling when he was stroked. It wasn't an aggressive thing, it was almost like a cat purring. Though he would never do it to me.

He was an instant hit with everyone including the cat and dog. He was so chilled out he would live all day in the house and all night in the kennel without a complaint.

This was probably like paradise to what he was used to. He straight away bonded and settled. It was like it was meant to be. I know many people say that dogs don't understand the rehoming and that it makes no difference to them after the first few days of settling in but every dog I have taken from a rubbish start have seemed to appreciate it. Whether it is appreciated or they just understand that this is better than before I don't know but I do know there is something that seems to enhance your bond in my experience.

I got started on him quite quickly with his training, I had some fun with him but in the fun I used to do a bit of training too. He would do anything for a ball and most of my training was done with one. He had an odd habit of getting very excited and chasing the ball but when he got it he would just drop it on the floor which usually meant I was getting fitter than him and certainly covered more miles in our games of fetch. See how they train you.

He would bite but he wouldn't let go. He would follow me around constantly looking for reassurance, there were very few times that his nose wasn't touching my hand. It was a lovely trait but did get quite annoying when you are spending more time wiping your hand dry from his nose than anything else. He had to be around me or at least in view and it all hailed from his insecurities.

He worked well for me but his confidence needed so much work. I took him to see Mick. I knew his confidence was low and he had nothing but adoration for me but anyone else including family he used to be nonchalant about.

I showed Mick how he would go in for the bite and Mick agreed it was a good bite but needed work to get him to release.

A bad bite or a bad experience around a bite is very real for a dog. It is a time when they are very focused and in their heads it is a very real thing and their adrenalin is pumping even in training and for them to undergo too much pressure or hurt themselves due to a bad baiter is as real as a car smash to a dog and can take a long time to get them over it. It bashes their confidence especially if their confidence hasn't been built up first.

A good analogy for them not releasing after a bite is if you were a door supervisor you will understand, or if you have fought in any arena. When the fight is done and you've got hold of the aggressor you take him outside holding on tight. If your confidence lacks you will not let go of him until help arrives, the reason for this is you don't know if you'll win again. If you let him go and he turns on you again, will you win this time?

Same as Polar, if he lets go he is not convinced he will win again. So he doesn't let go.

Confidence or lack of, drives this behaviour. There were more lessons to be learnt as well. As my Polar was hanging from Micks arm not letting go, I shouted "*OUT*" his command to drop off. Mick looked at me whilst struggling with Polar, "*is your dog deaf?*" me thinking this was a sensible question said "*no I don't think so*" Mick looked at me and said, "*why shout at him then*". The point is, it was his behaviour, his confidence. It wasn't through a lack of force in my command it was hard wired in his head to hang on in case he didn't win again.

In the short time that someone had attempted to train with him they had put too much pressure on him and now he was wary. The dog warden had said he would be a good security dog because when they tried to groom him he growled at them!! Such is the misconception of the industry, sadly its from within the industry as well.

With Micks help we started working on Polar and his confidence. I never told him off unduly just praised him for everything he did right. I played tug and let him win constantly. As he got the hang of it I would fight him more and more and put more pressure on him but he always won eventually.

I loved working him, he and I were so in tune with each other. He never really put a foot wrong.

He wasn't a challenge. He was gentle, kind and a really good friend. He loved nothing more than snuggling up with me or the kids.

I think with my loss of Max I really wanted this boy to do good. With what I had learned from Max and watching others, I could really see how to progress with Polar and his confidence. With his confidence built up he could really enjoy life without being as nervous. His nerves didn't show when I was working him, if he had to bark up he was pushing forward the whole time.

I worked with a person once who I will describe as a puritan. He didn't like the fact that Poley was white. He believed it meant he would be nervous and wouldn't be able to do the job. *"I'll push him back, whites are always nervous"* What he meant was with a bit of pressure Poley would give up tail between his legs.

I was told by my boss that I had to have him tested so they knew he wouldn't back off. Had I known then what I know now I would have told them to jog on but I was still trying to get ahead in this odd world full of pedigrees and ego's. So the next day I waited for her and her friend to arrive. After they had arrived on site and had a cup of tea explaining to me that because white GSD's came from a small gene pool they were inherently nervous. I wasn't and still am not sure if this is true. I have met as many balanced white GSD's as I have nervous ones. I don't really have an opinion on this except some are and some aren't.

So he decided on his course of action and he would start baiting Poley, gently at first by moving around suspiciously. Poley's interest was peaking as soon as he started swaying from side to side. Poley was intense and his stare never left, probably more wondering what he was doing than suspicious but then he shuffled forward and crossed Poley's line, Poley jumped forward barking and stood proud, his head cocked slightly the grumbling beginning and then erupting into a deep throated bark intermittently. He kept his eyes fixed and his posture rigid, his tail frozen and straight. The baiter moved forward and cracked a whip which sent Poley into a frenzy of teeth and loud barks. The baiter always staying out of striking distance for Poley b ut getting to close for his comfort, the whip cracked again but Poley never gave ground he just shuffled around aking sure he had a clear line to strike. This went on for a few minutes the posturing from both of them like two boxers circling each other, neither giving ground until the baiter shuffled forward, his movements becoming more erratic his posture straightening and squaring up to become more and more intimidating for Polar to see if he would back up. His shuffling became quicker and closer he was trying to make himself bigger to make Poley believe that he was taking on a bigger opponent but still Polar wanted to push forward. He wasn't giving an inch only getting angrier and more frantic until after a few minutes the baiter had to give up. Polar was not giving up anytime soon and it seemed that as intimidating as he could become without coming into range Polar was going to stand his ground. Chalk one up for the white GSD's. I couldn't hide the smug look from my face and the only ground the baiter would then give was that Poley must have been the *"exception that made the rule"*

One in the eye for him and a big smile on my face and extra treats for Poley.

Not long after that Poley and I moved on, I didn't particularly like the fact that I had to go through that because of one persons stereotype of a dog that had no grounding.

Poley worked with me on a beautiful prestigious golf club in Surrey. Acres and acres of land that was vandalised periodically by locals and kids. It had a really posh hotel which only had four rooms but a renowned restaurant. It was a peaceful site, no more cars screeching about and yobs trying to break in. Just the peace and serenity of acres of really pretty ground with some lovely staff who loved Polar.

Polar and I had some lovely times here, in the summer the scenery was quite breathtaking and in the quiet times you could find us in the walled garden just taking in the view and resting up.

Life at work had suddenly become relaxed with no threats or rushing around. No keys to hold or alarms going off. We used to patrol all night and the only thing we used to make sure we did was walk the staff to their cars through the dark just to make sure they felt safe. Poley used to get treats from one of the receptionist so he was always up for taking them to their cars.

I had worked there before to fill in shifts but now I went full time. It was perfect, Polar was coming on but not perfect and so it gave me loads of time to work with him.

I worked and trained with Polar for 18 months, he was great and was truly my dog. It was a selfish feeling but he would only work with me and he was constantly looking to me for reassurance, a trait of his nervous beginnings. But what a great dog just to be with.

His confidence was growing, his looking to me now was more of a habit than anything and I kind of liked it. I used to chat away to him and he was always attentive and never interrupted.

The golf course was acres and acres of uninterrupted beauty, not man made but man sculpted with rolling fairways and greens which at night was all mine and Polars to wander. Any season was beautiful there and especially in the mild summer nights where we could wander to our hearts content, train and play and as the sun went down I would find a lovely place to just sit and relax for a while. The staff were amazing and in the winter they would bring me out lovely stews and hot chocolate on occasion.

I remember working at the golf course one morning, my wife and I weren't really talking due to me always being at work and dog training. It was about 2am and was blowing a hooley, it was autumn time and the colours of the leaves were littering the floor and small tornados of leaves were being whipped up around the reception of the golf club so I decided I would take Polar for a patrol and enjoy some of the fresh cold air. I was walking towards the top of a hillock which was one of my favourite places to stand at the top and look out over Surrey and just think. The grass was long up there and Polar was snuffling around for scents of rabbit and deer that were frequently found bouncing around. The sky was so clear, the wind was blowing and the air seemed fresher than it had for days.

It was a beautiful spot and I was just looking across the scenery. Next minute Polar nudges under my hand by my side and I looked down, he looked up and I just thought to myself, why worry. In that moment everything came into perspective. It was amazing and 9 or 10 years later I can actually transport myself back to that.

Its an incredible feeling when you have those moments, maybe enlightenment, epiphany, I don't know how you would describe it. For me it was about being in the moment and realising that all the other garbage that clogs up your brain and your emotions. Actually not much matters. The life we have, most should be happy with and I can really only speak for myself as its all any of us can do.

But without the things that have happened to me, the mistakes I've made and the triumphs I have had all lead us to where we are now. Philosophy isn't what this book is about but if you have ever had a moment as I'm describing you will understand what I am getting at. If you haven't you have probably just been too busy to notice or there is one coming.

But if you have noticed, I for one still look back at these moments of which I have had a few and realise that whatever we do in life we end up where we are.

That may be an obvious statement. But all our mistakes are experiences, they lead us to where we are now and I for one wouldn't change a thing. And that is what I realised that night.

It gave me the strength to talk to my ex wife about leaving because I knew that whatever I did from there was the path I was taking and it was no good living in fear of what may happen and missing out on something that may happen.

It wasn't just that moment but that moment gave me an anchor point to remember all of this.

So now when I do get caught up in everything all I have to do is go out with my boy and surround myself with nothing but me and him. Peace and quiet and reflect. Reflect on what we have, not what we don't.

I have a loving family and three kids who I am hugely proud of though I probably don't tell them enough. I have an extended family, from my first ex wife that I would class as a good friend to a step son who is no longer my step son but I still have a relationship with because he was and still is part of my family. It is complicated, but in these moments it isn't. Because it isn't really.

I have family, my family consists of people who I am related by blood, by law, and just because they think the same of me. My Pack if you will.

This is part of the reason I relate to dogs so well because if you break everything down to the sum of its parts its all quite simple.

These moments remind me of this and the first of these moments was because of the peace Polar seemed to pass to me in that moment.

Its an amazing feeling and at the time was exactly what I needed to bring me back to earth and put all my woes back in perspective.

Polar gave me that moment.

It was a tempestuous time of my life with many uncertainties. On that particular night my soon to be ex wife had called a close to our marriage due to me never being at home.

My defence was the more hours the more money but I could never convince her, many of us have done the wrong things with the best intentions.

Dog handling had become a way of life and I spent a lot of time training, travelling and working away sometimes. I recall vividly talking to my Dad on the way home from a three day event having had no sleep. I was driving with a coffee and six energy drinks and a cigarette on the go constantly to stay awake. My Dad said *"that's great"* when I told him work was flowing in. *"You'll be the richest corpse in the cemetry."*

He was right, it has a name now. Work Life Balance, but now it has a name people don't take any notice of it.

For reasons of necessity right through to greed. I think when you have done a lot of hours to survive which is what I was doing, when you stop you appreciate it and understand all those people that said slow down and you didn't listen.

But at the time I couldn't have told you if working loads of hours was ruining the marriage or if the marriage was ruined so I was working loads of hours.

I think the most amazing thing I have ever discovered about dogs raised its head then. No matter who you are, what you're dealing with, how much money or possesions you have. Your dog will always be there. None of the material things matter. If you have their trust, respect and loyalty then they are going to be there through everything.

This is the moment I will always go back to when people ask me why dogs, I knew I loved being around dogs but until then I don't think I really knew why, and until then I hadn't had the chance to feel the calming nature and the simplistic nature that made them such wonderful companions.

That moment will always be etched into my mind because after that my wife and I did split up and I moved out with Polar into a house in Bracknell where I lived on my own apart from the times my children were over for the weekend and played with the sliding doors that were in the house, something I nor they will ever forget.

Polar never really liked being around anyone apart from me but I noticed that when I moved out and my stress levels were lower Polar stopped grumbling at everyone. He would curl up with my kids on the settee and really cuddle into them. His tolerance grew overnight and my bond with him got stronger.

Polar was beginning to gain confidence in his man work and releasing the baiter from time to time.

He still needed work but he was definitely going in the right direction.

Tragedy struck when I worked away for a few days at the Lord Mayors Show in Birmingham, there were a few of us there on overnight detail.

We positioned ourselves along the entrance road. I was working with a guy I had worked with a few times. He was further around the road from me and in between him and I were two dog handlers and in the compound was a lady with a couple of dogs, looking after the generators and other equipment.

To give you an idea of the level of people you would work with and to dispel the myth of glamour. Early hours of the morning myself and the other guy arranged to meet for coffee in the compound, so as I was in charge of the entrance I wandered up to the next gent along the road. As I walked up there was no movement, I could see his hi vis but he wasn't moving. I walked right up to his car and still nothing.

Polar and most dogs I knew would have been going mad at my presence but nothing from his car. I looked in the window and he was fast asleep with the hi vis pulled over him.

Shaking my head I walked up to the next car. It was an older guy and the same story, he was fast asleep in the drivers seat. I called down the radio to wake everyone up and alert them to the fact that we were going to take a break if they could look after our positions.

With a wry smile I wandered off towards the tea hut. This was the next challenge. The radio call had been unsuccessful in waking up the lady in the compound. We had to break into the compound and then break into the tea hut. The door to the tea hut was right next to the car that the lady dog handler was asleep in.

When we managed to get in apparently our voices woke her up. She got out of the car, looking a bit miffed and said "*what are you two doing*" I explained we were having a break and would she like a coffee? Her reply was brilliant. She said "*no thanks, I'll be up all night.*"

This is just one example of many. It was difficult to work with others some times due to standards and the different levels and what people thought was expected of them. With no regulation and no real base level of proffessionalism to start from, everyone seemed to do their own thing.

That very night we had a couple of lads try and get in through the gate and I used Polar to deter them, he was up on his back feet and barking away. Just how we all wanted our dogs to do. The lads thought better of it and disappeared. Whilst Polar was in mid flow and barking like a lunatic, I noticed a real difference in his behaviour.

Polar was an in your face type dog, the closer he could get the better and when he was rared up he would be right at the end of the lead. Teeth bared and putting on a great show of what he was going to do to you if you got closer.

68

Before he went forward you had to brace yourself, after a couple of lunges that night, he wasn't pulling as hard. He would go forward but at soon as the lead was taught he slacked off a bit.

When you work with a dog night in and night out, you really learn the mannerisms and body language. Although never to be mistaken for robots they do tend to do the same things in the same situations.

Polar was no different, so it was really easy to pick up on the fact he was in pain. Dogs rarely let you know it, to show pain in the wild would be to open themselves up to attack I guess. Survival of the fittest includes giving the impression of physical strength at all times.

So Polar. Bless his heart under threat from these two yobs continued to push forward and give the best account of himself he could, but I knew him so well. I could see it was all he had to give.

So when the situation was done and the lads had left I walked him away praising him as always for keeping Dad safe. When we were away and he had calmed down I noticed his left shoulder was stiff and his walking was slightly different.

Working dogs tend to have to be in a reasonable amount of pain before they let you know. All mine have anyway. It is the reason Hooch was affectionately named Tonka by Phil.

To think your dog is injured is a horrible feeling for most dog handlers because you put them in the situation.

They have done what they've done in defense of you and therefore you have a responsibility to make it right but also you carry the guilt too.

Although they live a great life and I truly believe a working dog is a happy dog, you do have to accept as with all dogs they may hurt themselves in the pursuit of their quarry, or just a ball.

So I rested him up for the evening, taking him for short walks so whatever he had done didn't seize up. I knew the next day we would be driving home and he could rest up.

We had done a couple of days on the show and it was quite exhausting work, so I was guessing he had just overdone it.

The next day we drove home, I kept an eye on his leg for the next couple of days but he seemed really uncomfortable.

Over the next couple of days his injury developed and on the third day tragedy struck, if you haven't heard a dog wail you won't understand. The noise is horrible, couple that with not wanting to go near their mouth because of their first instinct to pain is who is causing it? And then to possibly bite. Polar was in agony, he couldn't turn his neck, or move it at all.

I will remember that howl forever, it was blood curdling and again, there is nothing you can do. They look at you like you can take the pain away and you can look at not just the pain in their eyes but the lack of understanding and the pleading to stop it. All the while there is nothing you can do. Completely helpless.

It saddens me to even recount the story, it comes back to me and I will never forget those eyes. The eyes that locked on me when I first got him, the eyes that lit up when I opened his kennel, and the eyes that blazed brightly when protecting his friend. Me.

I managed to calm him down and carry him gently to the car. I drove him to the vets and he never moved. He knew to move would hurt. I knew in my mind it was bad. Dogs are so nosey but the whole journey to the vets he didn't once lift his head or even try.

My days are measured by the coming and going of your footsteps.

I anticipate them at every opening of the door.

You are the voice of caring when I am ill.

The voice of authority when I've done wrong.

At last at the vets he was in agony and the vet struggled to get near him, it was so traumatic, obviously for him but for me to watch and be completely useless.

The vet gave him painkillers and I was told to leave him with them and they would try and take away the pain and then do some tests.

Hours of restless waiting resulted in a phone call to tell me that he had a horrific reaction to the painkillers and now he was in agony and also really ill. The painkillers had loosened his bowels and made him really sick too because he had a reaction to it.

To rub salt in the wounds, he now had to have blood tests to see why the painkillers had caused such a reaction. But the whole time he had this problem with his neck. So the vets did what they could and I am sure there was a reason they went about Polar's treatment in the way they did. This went on for five days before Polar was finally strong enough to have an X- Ray on his neck.

It was a tense and horrible five days, I wasn't allowed to visit him because he was being kept as still as possible for obvious reasons.

Terrible news, the veterinary nurse phoned me. Polar was suffering from chronic arthritis and a progressive spinal problem. The barking up at the Lord Mayors Show had clearly brought the problem forward but from what the vet was saying it was a condition that had been brought on by the lack of shelter and nutrition in his former life as a stray.

The vet told me that its a huge problem with strays and malnourished dogs. But Polar was three years old, best guess and it just shows, he had been having great nutrition for the 18months I had been looking after him. So in those first 18 months his necessary nutrition and shelter had been so amiss that it had caused him permanent damage.

The vet said it would never get better, more than that , it would rapidly get worse. It was a condition that would fuse his vertebrae together to a point where he would not be able to curve his spine to turn or bend.

I still to this day struggle with the decision I had to make because it was so quick and our friendship was so short lived and it had to be. You don't have to like your path. It's just a path.

It was a horrible conclusion to what had been an amazing friendship. That's how I see my dogs, they are my friends.

There are so many cliche's about friendship, about how they don't judge, always be there for you, accept you for who and what you are. You could never see this so clearly as you do in dogs. It doesn't matter at all who you are, what you are, what you have, the mistakes you've made. They just know YOU.

After a day of contemplating things and everything the vet had said I picked my Poley up form the vets with a bag of pills.

I took him home, but it wasn't Poley. He was clearly in another world with the tablets and didn't really register peoples presence. Not even mine. When he looked at me there was nothing of him behind those expressive eyes. No real recognition..

The pain in his neck was so severe that he had to be on some pretty strong painkillers and they were dulling his senses. Even with the painkillers you couldn't go near his neck as he protected it from the pain.

I spent another three days with him before I decided to ring the vet. I spoke to a nurse who gave me her experience of dogs with this condition. It wasn't good, in the next six months he could potentially not be able to bend his body as his spine was fusing together.

He wasn't my Poley and he wasn't going to get any better. The tablets took away his personality and most of all I really couldn't stand to have him suffer any more.

I rung the vet and booked him in for his last appointment. I couldn't believe it had come to this. 3 dogs in as many years, loved all of them in different ways and started thinking this was not only not the job for me but I certainly didn't know how much more upset I could deal with.

It was like saying goodbye to a great friend every year. Polar was my greatest hope and he seemed healthy and young and vibrant until that night.

I said goodbye to Polar at a vets in Bracknell, Berks. I couldn't go in with him though I wanted to. He was very protective of me and it had to be a calm environment for him. I handed him to the nurse and gave him a cuddle and that was the last I saw of him.

The vet nurse walked back out with his lead and collar and I had to leave before I fell apart in public. I sat in my car for about 20 minutes, letting the tears subside and so I could think straight.

I remember vividly, when I turned the car on the CD player blasted Coldplay Violet Hill, right at the moment where he sang *"if you loved me, you should let me go"* Oh my god, I switched the car back off and fell apart for another 20 minutes. I still to this day can't listen to that song without thinking of my Polar, The first dog I really felt a true bond with.

It took a while for me to deal with Poley going, the problem with dogs and I guess any animals is they can't tell you what you are doing is right.

You can't get any confirmation that this is what they want you to do, I am sure many dogs go to early and many go to late because of this. You have to have the courage of your convictions and decide for them, its a hard decision that nobody explains to you when you get a dog you are going to be responsible for deciding when to end its life.

They can't and won't tell you how much pain they are in. They carry on as normal not letting anything show until they can't disguise it anymore. Then you know they are hurting but how much, is it enough to take their life for.

Poley couldn't tell me if he had enough, or if the pain was unbearable or if he wanted to live in a pill induced haze rather than go to sleep.

So you just have to best guess. I best guessed as many of us have, and hope I got it right and it was his time to go or I'm going to meet an angry Polar one day on the rainbow bridge as some people like to call it.

I don't know if I believe in all that but I do know I still talk to Polar from time to time because it gives me comfort, and to this day I believe I did the right thing for him. No animal or human should suffer like that with no way out. It was without a doubt one of the saddest days of my life and from time to time it still saddens me to think of him but for 18months he had the best life he could wish for and he left me with some beautiful memories which I will ever be thankful for.

The beautiful Polar Bear, too pretty for a working dog but a working dog he was and a great one.

This is Hooch modelling his serious face.

The Hooch

Hooch was about 1 1/2 years old when I got him from a pub in Four Marks in January of 2008, I remember vividly walking into the pub wondering what I was going to walk into.

I had been without Polar for about two months by now and I wanted to get back into working Dogs properly with my own dog. My ex wife and I had decided to give it another go, come what may, we had decided that if I did less hours it would improve our chances of working out.

Losing Poley had really taken the jam out of my doughnut and I was feeling a bit lost. I had been working a dog named Milo that a kennels had lent me.

The kennels that used to groom Poley before summer to sort his thick coat out and make him more comfortable. The kennels was run by a lady named Stella and she knew of Poley's fate. I had asked if she could keep her eye out for a new dog because she trained trials dogs.

She had rung me one day and asked if I wanted to look at Milo. He was not a young dog, but a dog handling company used to kennel him at her kennels and one day they had gone bankrupt and just never come back for him. He had been at the kennels for a few years.

Unfortunately he was too aggressive to attract new owners. She said he was fine with one owner if he bonded.

I went to see him, Stella said I could handle him for a while and make a decision. Stella brought him out. I looked in his eyes and my heart jumped a bit. More with fright than anything.

He was a big lad, his teeth were worn down and flat but he was a well kept good looking dog. He seemed to have a huge amount of sadness behind his eyes but with a fire that still seemed to burn bright when he stared right through me.

I wasn't sure, he actually made me quite nervous and I remember looking to Stella for some reassurance. *"He'll be fine, he just needs a firm owner"* Stella handed him over and I had a wander around with him, trying very hard not to show any fear. He was very intimidating. I decided I would try him.

I took him home and had a bit of time with him, I wouldn't let him around anyone because I really wasn't sure of him. Especially around other people.

I took him to work for a bit, every time I got him out of the kennel he would bark at anyone we encountered, adults, children, other dogs. It wasn't ideal.

I told my ex wife to leave him in the kennel while I was asleep and I would feed him and look after him. She decided she would feed him one day so I could have a lay in and came out of the kennel with teeth marks on her hand and stomach. He had to go back to the kennels.

So back to square one until I walked into the pub in Four Marks and met the owner Paul. Little did I know what a huge impact this trip would make to my life and everyone around me.

He took me up to his living quarters and I walked into his front room where a lovely little Rotti was asleep.

She didn't look up at me as I walked in so I made an instant decision. Objectively I need my dog to be inquisitive, if they don't look up when someone new walks into their territory they probably won't be any good as a protection dog.

I said this to Paul, tactfully. He said I'll bring Jerry Lee, clearly Paul had watched too many dog films. He was a big GSD with an edgy look in his eyes. He was allegedly an ex police dog. I say allegedly not in a doubtful way but as a dog handler nearly every GSD you meet is an ex police dog. Just like the disproportionate amount of people you meet in security that claim to be ex this and ex that.

I wasn't into him, he looked a bit too edgy, like one wrong move and he would be hanging of your arm. These are not dogs I look too. I could only think of Milo and his unsociable nature. I couldn't be having that again and I had learnt from the dogs I had that I wanted specifics this time. Not dog aggressive and entirely sociable but trainable.

My dog had to be good in a family environment, in a crowded environment because of the contracts I worked.

Teeth on a lead are not my thing. I said to Paul he wasn't my type of dog.

Paul rubbed his chin, he had to move one or possibly two of his dogs and as they were both trained protection dogs he thought one of these two would be my choice.

Paul said "*I have another dog but he's had no training and can be a real handful, shall I bring him in?*". Here was me hoping "*I love a challenge.*"

Paul left the room with Jerry. There was some scuffling and movement outside and a clear struggle. Then in ran a huge dog, he looked like a GSD but with floppy ears, and larger, bulkier, great looking dog. I remember looking inti his big doughy eyes and seeing the mischief behind them.

He jumped the coffee table knocking our drinks over, crashed into my 3 year old son knocking him over. His manic energy was incredible, he had no idea what he wanted to do. It was an unchanneled energy of the like I had never seen.

Paul spoke about how he hadn't been out with Hooch because of his energy and having to take three dogs all over 40kg out for a walk, Hooch and his dad had a fight where Hooch had done some damage to Jerry's ear.

I decided instantly that I wanted him. So much for "*it has to be the right one*", "*make an informed decision*" He was a bit like an unchanneled child. He had loads of energy but in his life he hadn't ever been asked to put into any order or direction, he had never been shown appropriate behaviour. So unchecked he was a 60kg K9 wrecking ball. But the positives were his potential was completely untapped, untrained and was like a blank canvass but with that amount of energy he would want and need training.

He got my vote that day, he reminded me of Scooby Doo. A lumux of a dog running about with no idea what he was doing and in my head I just thought of Lenny from of Mice and Men. But this one had fire in his belly and at this moment all he was looking for was mischief. He had a powerful build with a large head and a snout that was long like a GSD but wider and looked more powerful. The only thing you could really take from the Rotti was his powerful build and he had feet like a bear. He had a big black saddle and was slightly more tan than a GSD with a short ish coat.

The first time I met Hooch and I already had a voice for him. A deep slow voice like a slow version of Foghorn Leghorn for those of my age. That voice hasn't changed as he got older. It just got slower.

I have had voices for all my dogs. Don't know if its a common thing but I am not ashamed of it. I could assume a dogs voice for entire walks when I was out with the kids. Coming up with full blown stories of global domination. Such were our Sundays in Swinley forest with the dogs.

I told Paul I could collect him that Tuesday, I was off for the weekend and knew Hooch would take all my time and attention so I decided to have him the day I went back to work so I could get rid of some of that energy and get some manners into him before he was introduced to my family.

Oh my god, something is happening. I know something is because I saw a big bloke and a woman and a kid come up the stairs in the pub.

I was shuffled into the bedroom and left there with my dad, Jerry. I can hear them chatting away to Paul my owner. I can't quite hear what they are saying but I keep hearing my mums name Keira.

I know I'm going to stand near the door with my Dad. Its no good asking Dad, he's missing a bit of his ear. "Sorry about that dad"

Still can't hear. They are probably going to get rid of me. I've not been very good lately. I had a fight with my Dad, he still thinks he's the boss but I'm bigger than him now.

Ooh Ooh I can hear Paul coming, getting excited, whats happening, doors opening. I'm just going to stick my head out, ooh ooh ouch can't get my head out. Still going to try, no he wants Dad.

Right it's just me in the bedroom now. I wonder if they'll come and get me. If they are coming to take one of us it'll definitely be Dad, I mean Mum is lovely but she's really quiet. My Dad is really handsome, probably where I get it from hee hee. It won't be me. I can be pretty naughty and I'm a bit clumsy sometimes.

Paul's coming back, oh Dads back, hang on I'm getting pulled out of the bedroom. Looks like I'm going to get to meet them too woohoo. Paul has let go, off I go. I can definitely jump that table, oh bum bumped into the little one. Told you I was clumsy.

Not enough room in here with everyone, there go the drinks. That's my tail, nothing I can do about that. My tail is like a separate entity. Big bloke likes me I think. Keeps stroking me, I do like a stroke.

I'm going to sit next to him as he seems to like stroking me. It would be nice to get away from here.

All I do is stay in all the time, it gets boring after a while. Hang on, stair gate is open. I can definitely make that and down to the kitchen for that chocolate cake. Haha made it. Oh bum, didn't take the stairs well. Still ahead of them though. I can definitely make the kitchen. I can hear them running behind me haha. Got the cake, damn they got me, I can just swallow it. Done. In trouble, don't care. Im going back upstairs, Paul is holding me pretty tight, don't blame him.

Big bloke is laughing, at least someone found it funny.

This is a good day, I don't mind being in trouble. Adds to my charm. Big bloke still seems to like me, little one does too. He likes stroking me too.

They're going, oh what did I do. Was it the cake?

So all of my warnings to myself and my pontification was for nought. I found a dog, liked him, got him. I spent a lot of time between seeing him and the Tuesday I was picking him up wondering what the hell I had done. All of my assertions of checking him with other dogs and seeing if he was strong mentally had gone out of the window and actually I was very excited and slightly apprehensive. Apprehensive because this Dog Handling hadn't gone so well for me and even worse for my previous dogs but most of all did I have the knowledge and support to train a dog from green. Not just any dog but Hooch. I remember going to Four Marks on the Tuesday to collect him and having to lift him into the boot, he was 60kg when I got him, really overweight and a big unit to lift into my 4 x 4.

I didn't pay a penny for Hooch, Paul just wanted him to go to a good home, in fact he came with a free bag of food.

Hooch was not sure what was going on having never been in a car before and Paul was really upset about letting him go.

You see Paul had nothing but love for Hooch but I think deep down he knew he hadn't given Hooch the start he needed, he loved him but love isn't enough.

You can like or love something, someone but if you don't give them what they need the love is pointless. He was holding Hooch back and he knew it but wasn't in a situation to do anymore than he had for him. He had kept him fed and brushed and healthy apart from his weight but this isn't enough for a dog.

In fact all of Paul's extended family were in love with Hooch and sorry to see him go. I had a photoshoot done with Hooch for my 40th, no laughing. When the lady posted the pictures on her photography social media site a friend of hers got in touch asking if it was Hooch. You will have to forgive me if the family are reading this as I have forgotten the family dynamics.

We had a good chat and she got me in touch with the lady that now owned Hooch's sister. We arranged to meet up when Hooch was about 8 and we met at a lovely forest that I used to take Hooch to called Tweseldown in Surrey.

Here is a picture of the two of them Hooch is on the left.

I remember Cesar Milan saying dogs need exercise, discipline and then affection and whatever your views on him, he's not wrong. You can love a dog as much as you like but without boundaries, regular exercise you will never fulfill their potential.

Potential is what a dog is all about, they don't need self help books and pep talks, they just need pointing in the right direction. You see dogs truly are the masters of adaptation, they will be whatever you want them to be, more importantly they will be whatever makes them an integral part of the pack.

Hooch until now had run wild but I knew in him he had the potential to be an amazing dog to train in whatever I wanted him to be because he had the energy, he loved the attention, and he definitely had the brain.

Hooch was sat in the back of my 4x4 and I was chatting to Keith telling him I had collected him. Trying to describe how he looked and how big he was and mainly what i saw in him. Keith has always been supportive, he is a straight talker but he knows when something matters to you and tries to help. He was giving me advice on what to do first and how to bond.

I had gleaned a lot of information from training and having the other dogs I had but it was always good to learn new ideas or be reminded of ideas that you have forgotten over time now there is a life lesson.

In my chatting I forgot that Hooch hadn't been in a car before and on my way home I stopped to get the car washed in this great auto car wash, like the American ones that pull you through. I was halfway through it when I looked in the back and Hooch was captivated, he was staring at what was going on outside. I remember thinking, he'll be alright. This hasn't phased him what will.

I'm trying to have a kip, whats all that banging. Can you beleive it, Paul is packing up my stuff. My food too, what the hell. Put that back. This is because I broke the toilet door, I told you Paul I was scared that someone was breaking in while you were in the loo.

Oh hang on, there is that big bloke again. He keeps looking at me funny, I wonder what he's thinking. I reckon he'd be alright as a new owner. Seems to have a decent smile, tickles my ears. I think he has potential. If he really knows what he's doing you can really train these humans to do almost anything.

Its just about the way you treat them, giving them enough attention and showing them those PDSA eyes. He'll be a pushover..

He's opening the boot of his car, I think he wants me to get in. Haha training starts here. Lets see you lift me big man, I know I'm not as slim as I have been but there's no need to groan, and whats that vein popping in your head.

And we're up, knew you could do it. Lets see if we can get you doing that all the time.

Cars quite comfy and big, don't remember being in one of these before.

I was just pondering life and its many intricacies when the car started to slow. I was just thinking how nice it is just sitting in the back watching the world go by. It would be nicer to get a bit closer to the trees, maybe have a sniff.

Oop he's turning in, whats this big building. Maybe this is his garage, looks odd. Oh MY GOD what is going on, big bloke!! BIG BLOKE!! Something is shooting water at us, what the hell are those massive erm erm brushes I think.

Oh god not foam, theres foam. This is freaking me out, think of those trees we drove past mmmmmmmm trees lovely green trees. Oh god make this stop.

So it begun, to make a silk purse from a sows ear. I was quite captivated by him, I took him home and let him run around in the garden for a while.

He was like a kid in a candy shop. He had an issue. He was quite nervous to begin with. Until he had explored the garden fully he was quite hesitant. More than quite hesitant. He sniffed everything from afar before taking a closer look and sniff. The whole time his eyes were darting around keeping an eye for danger or movement. His eyes would look from me to the gate and back door, always on the move. I put it down to new areas and new smells. I got ready for work.

This would be the beginning of his training. Dogs adapt very well and especially if you use association. When I'm in uniform Hooch would learn we were going to work, a collar for work a collar for leisure. This way he would always be ready when I was in uniform and he had his work collar on.

It takes time, a lot less than you would think but it does take time. People who know dogs understand how quick you can train them, you can teach them bad habits just as quick as good. Dogs can train people just as quick as we train them if you're not careful. One thing I have always instilled in my dogs and have found it invaluable over the years is that inside the home is calm and relaxing. I know this can be difficult with puppies and young children but if you look to later on in their lives if indoors is the place to play you will never have any peace. If you make indoors relaxing for them and try and keep play for outdoors it becomes their sanctuary as much as it is yours. Hooch has always abided by this and at eight stone in a two bed house or a mobile home it was invaluable.

Well, we got home, those brushes didn't swallow us. Wow that freaked me out.

Anyway were safe now. Me and this bloke, I've sussed out his name is James.

He seems to be happy and the woman and the little person are here to but I am quite clearly meant to be with James most of the time as he sat in the garden with me and fed me. It was nice playing in the garden with him, then he put me in this house thing with a bedroom and a outdoor space.

I hope they don't think that I'm sleeping in there

He then came out of the house with a uniform thing on and put a collar on me.

Clipped a lead on me and showed me the way. I wonder where we are going?

He got to the back of the car, here we go. I'll stand fast, he can lift me again haha.

Is that ham I can smell, I love ham, its in the car. Up I go, got to get the ham. Damn the boot shut, he got me in. I'll get him next time. In he gets with a big smug smile on his face. I've noticed he rarely stops talking.

Off we go for another drive, I'm getting used to this.

I went to work, at the time I was working for a Russian gentleman in Weybridge. I was contracted to look after his family home and it was a lovely job for a dog handler, a nice dry warm log cabin to sit in which the dog could stay in with you.

The contract required walking around his property of which there were several acres. Rarely bumped into any of the family and loads of land to tire the dog out in.

There was room to play ball and the land was beautiful. Loads of opportunities to train, different surfaces and noises and animals. All good for environmental training.

Environmental training is as important as any other form of training. To teach a dog that they can walk across any surface or through anything. It is about confidence again.

You cannot train for every eventuality but you can arm them with as much knowledge as possible. It is unrealistic and to time consuming to take them out on every surface you can think of and every situation you could encounter.

So you attempt to get them walking in and through all sorts of different situations. Gravel, stones, mud, stairs water, trees, wind, fireworks. You start with the most common and try and build on it.

I guess fireworks are the ones that get many dogs. As an example, I used to work fireworks night at a big event every year.

As a result Hooch now watches fireworks with curiosity not fear. When we were at bonfire night we used to stand at the back of the crowd and I would put him in a down while I watched the fireworks, I thought it was important for him to understand that if I would stand and watch them there was no harm to come. He never really reacted to them and we now both enjoy them together.

If you pay too much attention you can easily cause a larger problem.

It's very similar to when your son or daughter falls over and it isn't too bad, you pick them up and dust them down and make little of it.

If you do make something of it, you will find the child will now make a lot more of it than you wanted and it becomes a huge situation.

It wouldn't have if you hadn't given any attention, as humans, especially children and many adults I know on social media they love a bit of attention, so as soon as you show that it is worthy of attention it becomes worthy of all of your attention. For quite a while usually.

If you pay too much attention you can cause anxiety in the dog because they believe you are worried too. Now its a problem.

Its not much different from children, if they have positive experiences with all the new situations they encounter then a result of this is that they will be much more willing to enter into new experiences.

Again, you cannot show children how to handle every new experience they will have in their lives but you can equip them with a plethora of positive outcomes from the experiences they do attempt.

We encountered our first wobble at work the very first night.

We were wandering around as was my job. I make light of it, as a dog handler we did a lot of wandering but we called it patrolling.

As you become used to the job, observation becomes second nature. It may look like a wander but actually were taking it all in and because you constantly work outside you become very used to the dark, my night vision used to be amazing.

Since leaving the job this has deteriorated incredibly. But at the time and for all the dog handlers out there you get so used to working with no light that you really can see in the dark. Also your sense of smell heightens because out there at three &four in the morning there is nothing to smell but the night itself, I have found myself noticing deodorant, coffee. Cigarette smoke is an affront to the senses when you are out there on your own in the middle of the night.

But the biggest advantage you have whilst out there is that when you are really in tune with your dog he will notice everything and you will notice him noticing everything.

That first night, after I had lost my Polar and I really truly trusted him to tell me everything that was going on, his ears would go up and if it was people he would air scent and if it was animal his nose would go straight to the ground, you see when you work with dogs they really are your eyes and ears and you notice everything because sometimes when you are in a charged environment where people could come out at you they are your guardian.

There are jobs where you rely solely on your dog for all your information and early warnings.

Like I say with Polar I knew and had relied on for a couple of years and it was this night it suddenly hit me that I didn't have my safety blanket anymore.

Polar would kick off at strangers in the night, teeth and spit and I could rely on him to do so.

I was walking around with Hooch and he had his head down, sniffing and checking, he didn't have a clue and why should he, he's never been in this environment. But his instincts drove him to do what his instincts drove him to do so he was sniffing. I couldn't expect him to pick up on things and if he did, would I pick up on him picking up on things, his signals would be completely different, he didn't even have stick up ears to watch. Oh jees, this was a mistake. Hooch was loving his time, just enjoying walking around and checking out his new environments.

The gardener walked towards me. He was a lovely guy from New Zealand, he knew a bit about working dogs but mainly collies and cattle herders. He had grown up on a farm in New Zealand and never tired of telling me his little anecdotes about the vast areas of land and his possom hunting in his youth.

Chris knew I had got a new dog and was eager to meet and befriend him as he had all of Polar. As he walked over he said *"Wow, GSD x Rotti more like X pit pony. Look at the size of him."* As he walked up Hooch looked apprehensive and disappeared as best he could behind my legs. My heart sank. What happened to the energetic full on dog I had seen. Where was the friendly mischevious boy that had welcomed everyone he had met so far. I wasn't sure how to approach this, I tried to coax him out to meet Chris but he just didn't want to know. There was no aggression but I couldn't tell by his eyes what was going on. It seemed a mixture of sadness and apprehension. Hooch wouldn't go near him. He sank back and stayed there and no amount of coaxing or Chris kneeling down making himself smaller, trying to get his attention would make Hooch acknowledge him.

This is when I started doubting myself, kicking myself for not testing him and checking. But what I saw was there, I knew it was it just needed help in coming to the surface.

Well this is lovely, we had arrived somewhere. Trees and lovely gardens and a lovely cabin with a bed to sleep on. I can smell all the other dogs. We must share it, oh great other dogs other than mum and dad. This could be great.

James took me out for a walk, he kept talking to me but I have no idea what he's saying, he seems happy about it though.

86

The smells are lovely, I don't know what they all are because I've never smelt some of them before. James keeps pointing at stuff. Stopping and listening. Not sure if I'm supposed to follow suit? Oh well enjoy it while I can. Of course I would enjoy it but James won't let me stop where I want to, he only lets me stop where he wants me to. Selfish

As we're walking around this guy starts walking towards us. He's smiling but I don't know if I like him. I'm going to hide behind James, I don't like him. I'm not going to him. James Is looking at me oddly, I think he's a bit disapointed but I'm not going to him. I don't even know him. I'm going to stay right here behind James because I just don't like the look of him.

I left it at that and walked away from Chris and back on patrol with a really bad feeling nagging at the back of my mind. I left it because at this point and with his confidence low I didn't feel it was right to put any pressure on him, I didn't want to make him do anything he didn't want to. My plan was to have fun with him and introduce him to this new world with fun involved. It was no good shouting at him or forcing him to meet someone he clearly didn't want to.

What if, what if I couldn't do anything with him and what if my instincts were completely wrong about this boy.

Luckily for him and I think for me, I had been really taken by him just in a few hours he was already looking up at me for guidance and had the most amazing temperament, when walking on patrol he had a grace and a composure that put him head and shoulders above many dogs literally and metaphorically.

Most young dogs have a roll to their shoulders, as opposed to a certain strut as they get older and are more sure of themselves when they begin to place their feet.

When dogs are young they seem to have less sureness to their walk. Their shoulders roll and they they place their feet softly as if not to be noticed by other dogs. I believe it is just a sign of immaturity.

As they get older they place their feet with a sureness, maybe its for balance or just as people do they enter a group of other dogs or people to make an impression so as people puff their chests out and stand up straight dogs have a meaningful walk and attempt to show the group that they have a certain position in the pack.

Hooch had this lovely skulking gait, it was almost a stalk when he was looking forward. His shoulders still rolled but it was almost predatory.

When you are using a dog for protection the approach to a situation is as important sometimes more important than any other part of the situation.

Hooch had a natural swagger and with his head up I could imagine he would be quite intimidating, if only I could make his heart as strong as his swagger.

I have found this in many Rotti's I've met, I know they have a reputation and in some cases they are deserving of it but in a huge majority you can look them in the eye and see that they are as in need of your love and attention as any other dog.

They would never show anyone that apart form their nearest and dearest. Rottis are like the true macho man, if they were to watch Marley and Me they would be crying their eyes out but no one is to know.

This is the impression I got from Hooch, he is a big macho dog but underneath nothing but a softie.

The first couple of nights I concentrated on getting to know him, playing ball and spending time.

Making sure he knew boundaries but no shouting or harsh behaviour. I was worried that his confidence couldn't take too many hits. I was only going to have to build it up again anyway.

What a great time I had, I kind of forgot his initial nerves with Chris and just enjoyed his company. I think he was enjoying the freedom, at first he was really wary of open space and wouldn't leave my side but as he got used to it he opened up.

He was a loyal one man dog, you could tell that with next to no time with him. I remember trying to tire him out and it wasn't working so I met a couple of Dog handler friends who were at very high standards with their dogs. They were working near me and I recommended a kennels that had an agility course for hire near me.

The agility course was owned by a lovely lady Stella. We hired the course and met up.

My friends came over to say hello to Hooch in his cage and Hooch couldn't make himself any smaller. He instantly retreated to the back of his cage and looked to me with eyes that could melt my heart. My god, he was so unsure of everything, it didn't look like fear in his eyes. It looked like a plea "what shall I do" One of my friends looked at me and said, "*you got a nervous dog there*"… Last thing I wanted to hear, but I still maintain it wasn't nerves.

You have to remember and empathise a little bit.

His entire life had been shaken, not like a puppy. Hooch had spent all his life with the same people and in the same few rooms.

So far I had wrenched him out of this, for long term benefit but dogs don't see that. Dogs adapt, there is no real happy or sad situation, there is just the situation.

Hooch was now in a situation that he hadn't encountered before with the only person he knew being me and he didn't even know me very well. I had taken him from the only world he knew with the only people he knew and put him in this vast world, his eyes hadn't opened yet to the beauty of all of this freedom.

He was so lucky but he didn't know it yet and as such he cowered from it.

I put this to the back of my mind and just had some fun over the agility, Hooch isn't built to be agile but he did OK on small jumps, couldn't fit his feet on the high walk and didn't get the tunnel at all.

But in the hope that his confidence would grow there was no telling off only rewards and happy voices to make him feel like it was a great place to be.

The disparity kept hitting me between the sheer size and bulk of him and the puppy like behaviour. The sad looks and the completely lost looks. The only way to put it into an analogy is my son is 12 and nearly 6', as you can imagine people don't treat him like he is 12 they treat him like he is 6'. Hooch was the same it was so difficult to remember he wasn't much more than a year old.

Does this bloke ever give it a rest. I've been at his "work" wandering around all night and rather than go and get breakfast were at some other place. It seems ages since I ate, when did I last eat?

So here are another couple of his friends, more people I don't know. For gods sake, what is it with him showing me around like a trophy. Oh they are coming over. Get to the back of the cage, I don't know you "SOD OFF". I'll shoot James a look, maybe he'll understand and get rid of them. I'm not happy with strangers. I know the people I know and that's enough.

Oh, so out we go. I'm feeling a little bit tired not sure what we're doing next.

James is taking me to an area that's all fenced off. Oh he's having a laugh isn't he. Agility!! I'm not built for this sort of stuff. I don't even fit in that ridiculous tunnel. What is the point of this.

James seems to be enjoying himself though. His voice is all high pitched. Ahhh, he's really enjoying himself. He seems happier when I follow him around and it makes him really happy when I jump.

This is actually quite good fun, when he says "up" it means I have to jump over the thing that were running at, like I wasn't going to haha. Oh well it makes him happy.

I'm still pretty hungry though.

So we had a great time at the agility and the more and more I did with him the more he was looking to me, I think in these moments of insecurity which most dogs have when you rescue them from what they know however bad, they have no idea who you are so when you are the only one they can look to is when the bond starts developing and this is what was happening with Hooch.

Over the next few days I really tried to take the energy from him. His energy seemed endless. I took him to work Tuesday night, agility Wednesday, work Wednesday night, training Thursday, work Thursday night. He was still full of energy on Friday. I never expected such a big dog to have so much energy. I can only guess he didn't want to sleep with all of these new experiences going on.

He still seemed nervy but that wasn't going to heal itself anytime soon,. I thought when we got into the routine of work and sleep and he got to know everyone and everywhere he would build in confidence.

As time moved on he really started to look to me more and more, he met the family but his comfort zone was always in sight of me. I played with him and found he had a huge love for the ball.

This was great, easy way to get him and keep him fit; also it serves well as a drive for training. I used the time I had at my Russian boss's to really get him on point, this never happened.

Due to Hooch's size it didn't matter how sharp you tried to make him in his obedience it didn't ever look sharp. To get him from in front in a sit to the heel position in a sit seemed to take minutes, you could watch other people with their 25kg Belgian Malinois and before the command had left the handlers mouth they were in a lovely sharp sit, Hooch would still be getting himself comfortable for what seemed like a couple of minutes after the command.

I would carry on working on that I thought. Agility, not really his cup of tea. He was always happy to do it and seemed to enjoy it but was more at home putting his head down to run through things than jump over them. He never really disobeyed but I guess at his size, sharp obedience and agility were never going to be his strong points.

These disciplines were really only to help him overcome demons and to help him understand my role as alpha and also it's great to bond with a dog if you make all this fun, your value goes up in their heads like a child. If you buy your son a ball, to really enjoy that ball he has to interact with someone, buy him a PlayStation or Xbox and he no longer needs you or anyone else. Don't get me started on that.

90

Wow, this man thinks he's going to beat me. Does he not know us dogs can go on forever. And I for one am much better at endurance than a sprint.

James will run out of new things to do before I run out of energy. Silly man.

I have to say I am getting tired, this is my third day on the go. It's all new and it's amazing, I've learnt to sit and stand. Hang on!! He's training me. I did not even notice. That was clever, he was dressing it up as fun but I'm learning. It's ok learning like this though.

We've been all over the place and to loads of new places. Just me and James, it's starting to feel like a fit now between us. He never shouts or loses his temper. I'm never cooped up with other dogs, it seems like it's just going to be me and him. That would be a bit weird!!

I'm not overly happy with the whole kennel situation, when we do go home, I seem to get dumped in this kennel they call it and left there on my own. Then they let this other dog out called Oscar who wanders about free, sometimes he even pees up my kennel and then goes back in the warm.

Anyway I can't really complain, James is doing a good job. Especially of training me without me knowing it ha-ha, wait until I tell!! Who, who am I going to tell. It's just me in this kennel thing.

Oh well maybe things will change. Not too much though. I kind of like him. I miss my mum and dad. Sometimes it makes me a bit sad, my old life was cool and lazy. Life here is kind of full on I do enjoy the training though.

In fact I did get loads of attention today at a training place and I did get to pull a guy about with a tug. That's my favourite game, showing people how strong I am.

I play it with James but I don't want to hurt him. This new guy thought he could win, I got four wheel drive and a low centre of gravity. You got nothing on me. I think I might grab a few winks while I can.

Do not chastise me unduly for I am your right arm.
The sword at your side.
I attempt to do only what you bid of me.
I seek only to please you and remain in your favour.

Hooch and I were becoming a team, not a team to be reckoned with, but a team all the same. He was great and I had a great time with him when we were training and things.

When you are training a dog to be a Protection dog, you aren't really training them per say. All you are really doing is nurturing their instincts.

Something else that I'll remember for my management book. You nurture what they already do.

You see a dog can bite, a dog can bark, a dog can sit, stand, lay down. It can do all of these things, what we do is train the dog to do it all to a command. Also probably more importantly, only on command.

When teaching your dog the commands and that he/she is to bite on command you must teach them first a command to let go. All of these things you teach on tugs, rags, towels.

The point I am making is you always use the same words in training, because it is the command that is important. Your dog already has the ability to do all of these things, you are purely giving him a word, a sound really that is connected to him doing it.

Also it has an added benefit; if the dog does something off his own back like lay down you can say "down, good boy" it's all association.

Association and common sense, it can be a way of making a difficult dog quite subservient. Just by telling him the command and good boy, you don't have to instigate it, just acknowledge it.

Hooch had a way of understanding me that was strange, it's like we were on the same wavelength all of the time.

Part of this understanding came from his attention, he was aware of me and where I was at all times. In fact most of the time he was watching me. This made things a bit easier. I found it very easy to teach him with hand signals.

I remember on the Russian gents house there was a fork in the path, it didn't matter which way you went you could still cover the entire grounds. But as in all security you break routine, routine is bad if you are patrolling. It is never as good idea to advertise to the people you are protecting the customer from where you will be and when. So sometimes you went left, sometimes right. Break your routine, keep them guessing. This took Hooch two night shifts. I would say "this way" and point to which path I was going down. When I said "this way" he would look and then the point would be the cue. This became a thing, we would always get there and he would look.

Now when out on walks with him, if we get to a junction, he looks at me waiting for which way, I say "this way" and point.

Dogs love routine and repetition is the way to train but obviously you have to do it in new places to make sure it's not just in one place he will do it.

So Hooch and I continued with this, but with his constant attention it was made so easy.

Well, this isn't weird. I told you about the training right? He's been training me covertly. While I'm mucking about having fun, he's been getting me to sit while I wait for the ball, or bark before he throws it. I do it because I want him to throw the ball, then halfway down the field I realise what he's done.

It's like Jedi mind tricks, the sneak. Now if I lay down, he tells me to lie down, but afterwards. What does that mean? I'm going to have to watch this one. Paul used to give me treats, I always knew if he was going to try and train me because he'd go and get some cheese, then he would show me the cheese, let me sniff it, then tell me to do something.

What was wrong with that way, I knew what was happening then. Now I see the ball, get all excited, sit, down, bark whatever then I'm chasing the ball again. He's not going to be easy to disobey this one.

Still it's a lot of fun, I love the ball. When I was at Paul's I just used to rip them up. I didn't know you could chase them too. It's great. It goes so far and I can really get some speed up. Takes me a while to stop, my brakes don't always work as well as I think they do. It's tiring..

I did have to laugh the other day, James put me in my kennel, it's getting to be every day now and I'm not happy about it, so I thought I'd make a stand. He pointed and said "in" all happy as if it was a good thing, I put on my best posture and wouldn't move. "IN" he said, quite sharply. I've never heard him get stroppy. I did not move. He held my collar and walked in to the kennel, I went with him, he said "stay" and as he tried to get out I barged past him and back in the garden. Ha-ha, you should have seen his face. He pulled me about for a while, tried to get me to stay but every time he left the kennel so did I. I ended up left in the garden. Ha that'll teach him. Don't mess with Da Hooch.

After a week I encountered his first bit of stubbornness today, I guess he was getting used to me. I had tried to put him in the kennel and the little sod wasn't having any of it. I thought the kennel would be a bigger problem sooner to be fair. He was stubborn, you tend to find bull breeds and the like quite stubborn dogs, and they try and prove who the leader is quite regularly. This was the first time for Hooch, until then he had done so well.

He took to all the training and exercise like he had always done it. We were only a few days in and he had been perfect. I knew there would be obstacles and this was the first.

After a night shift, one of the last things you want to be doing is trying to convince your dog to go to bed, but that's exactly what was happening. Hooch would go in the kennel but as soon as I made a B line for the door so did he. It's pretty frustrating and after the week of trying to tire him out I was absolutely shattered.

It was a lesson learned. I gave up too soon. He was hard work. But however hard it gets you must remain consistent. This is what I learnt from this debacle. But for now I decided to go to bed and figure it out tomorrow. I knew the kennel would be a challenge having never been in one before. Other than that it was going like a dream.

The next day, I spoke to my then wife. He was getting on with everyone in the small trials we had done, Oscar was no problem, Hooch had paid little or no interest to the cat and he was fine with Ryan.

So I walked in from work and straight into the house like nothing was different. Put his food down in the kitchen. It took him a while to get there, he had to sniff everything. So far so good, he was cool.

The cat was looking at him from half way up the stairs and Oscar was just running around between his legs. Thumbs up, little did I know.

Ha-ha, it worked, I won. I'm indoors, he clearly doesn't want round two of kennel gate. So here I am. I am going to claim the big sofa, looks comfy. I'll have dinner first. This little dog needs to get out from under me and that cat. I saw him looking, he will make a great chase partner. My world is complete.

After dinner I decided to have a nap. It was nice, James wouldn't let me on the sofa, just a matter of time.

The cat food was tasty, it's all very relaxed in here.

Oops, there is something in the garden, Oscar is off. I'm off to. He can fit through the table and chairs, I can't they are coming with me. Ha-ha, this is great.

What a life, me and Oscar can chase birds and stuff out of the garden. James is coming, hopefully he'll get this chair of my back so I can chase the birds properly.

He does not look like he's coming to help. Oh god, he's got the hump. Chair is off, here we go the kennel is being opened again. Ha-ha James is calling me, like I'm going to fall for that. Errrr nope. Come on Oscar lets go back in.

Back door is shut, Oscar is in, I think James wants' a word. Maybe I shouldn't have messed about on the first day. I'm still not going in that kennel. He's got me by the collar. Here we go, didn't he learn yesterday.

Oh wow, I think he's got the proper hump, he just dragged me to the kennel, I guess that's it for indoors for today. He's not getting me in here, he's trying to push me in, and he's quite strong. It's because he's a bit lumpy. He puts his weight behind him and he's got the advantage. Dammit, brute strength and he won. Let's see what happens tomorrow. I'm not letting this go.

This day was a massive wake up call. I think we can all agree that one time in our lives we have believed too much in our ability or instincts and we are soon put straight by family, friends, pets or worst case scenario people that exploit it as if it is a weakness but it's just a human condition.

I let him in too soon, I didn't really know him though I was completely taken by him I shouldn't have let this blur my expectations. He was still a dog and dogs will push the boundaries when given the chance. He did.

I heard all of this crashing around downstairs and my wife of the time shouting.

I sprung out of bed and ran downstairs to find Hooch running around the garden, the dining table and chairs scattered on the way to the door, and one chair had even made it outside. Hooch looked like he was having the time of his life. Chasing around the garden, Oscar was looking like he had done something wrong and was skulking around. He knew the rules, Hooch had no idea. He was bounding around as if this was just a normal activity and with his strength and size he was leaving quite a wake.

Hooch was taking no notice at all. But then I guess he didn't know he had done anything wrong.

I recall being told years ago about house training a dog. He said if your dog goes to the toilet in the house, you should roll a newspaper up and then hit yourself over the head with it.

The point is, most indiscretions by dogs are caused by the owners neglect.

Dogs are opportunists. By that I mean they react to situations. They have very little or no care as to consequence. They just grab the moment. If you allow them these opportunities they will take them. This is what I had done,

I had allowed Hooch to think he was in charge by letting the kennel thing go and then rewarded him by allowing him the privilege of coming indoors and taking the proverbial.

I grabbed Hooch's collar, I hadn't been angry with him so I guess it came as a shock to him. He followed although he had a stubborn side like most dogs and every couple of steps dug his feet in. It took some doing but I managed to drag and pull him into the kennel and straight away he turned around. He set his feet, his head dropped lower and he stared at me with an intensity I hadn't seen before. It was a challenge and it was a challenge I had to win. He had a stubborn look in his eyes, it was almost like he was rolling his sleeves up. He moved to walk out, I stood in his way, and he moved to go round me. I pushed him back and he straight away leant his weight into me and pushed back, it was like a sumo match and I for sure could not fail. I had to show Hooch consequences. I had to prove to him that he couldn't do as he pleased.

I won this match and it took a lot out of me. I was pushing him back in the kennel for no more than a couple of minutes but it sapped my strength. Hooch was strong and slippery as an eel. I was worn out but I had to win, this was Hooch's first harsh lesson.

It wouldn't be his last, I knew that but it was important for him to understand that I was still the boss and all the fun he was having was contingent on him behaving. I know dogs don't think like this but they do understand patterns of behaviour. I do this, I get this!!

That's all they need to know and it works, consistency along with repetition.

I went back to bed, with this on my mind and making an oath to myself that I would take this as a lesson learnt. From that day forward I had to show Hooch the boundaries.

It's funny because I had defied a belief of mine, I always tell people when getting dogs, puppies or rescues. The dog must adapt to you not the other way around. You and your family carry on doing what you do and the dog learns to work around it. Nothing proves this point better than a puppy that has been brought up with children. Children can be unpredictable. Lots of children can be a dog's worst nightmare, but when the dog has been brought up around them they cope with it just fine. Hooch has never really been around children running around and playing. My son was always a calm child at home and there was only him. If Ryan had friends over or my daughters were over, Hooch tended to take himself somewhere quiet. Hooch wasn't a problem around kids but he clearly wasn't comfortable around them so he used to take himself away and the kids were instructed to leave him alone. My brother has two young children and a younger British Bulldog called Betsy. Betsy has never known anything other than kids running around her and is more than happy to join in on the fun. During children's parties she can often be found in the same room as the disco or party games fast asleep. She is completely desensitised.

This is because it's perfectly normal; the dog has had to deal with it and with no alternative knows nothing else.

If you aren't going to allow your dog on the furniture, don't allow him/her on the furniture. Not ever, not because they are lonely away from their siblings, not because fireworks are going off, dogs adapt, it's what they do but there is nothing harder than adapting to something that keeps changing.

I get many people ask about what to do with puppies, as for all dogs, you do what you want to do and they work around you. There are exceptions, but if you don't have the fortitude to listen to a puppy howl for a couple of nights, dog owning is maybe not for you.

I have worked and trained rescue dogs and all I have ever done is what I wanted to do and what I wanted them to do. Sounds harsh doesn't it? But you don't have to do it with cruelty.

You see I sussed out what to do with Hooch and the kennel situation. I wanted him to be in the kennel, for his own good. It was to rest up and feel fresh by the evening. I had a son who wouldn't leave him alone, a cat who constantly badgered him to play and a wife who was in and out. The best thing for him so he could do his job was for complete rest for as long as I rested. So if I could get him in the kennel, he could have his dinner and rest undisturbed and then when I got up he could come out and have family time that was the plan.

I have mentioned that dogs think simply. To outthink a dog, you should always try to think simply as well. The clue was there, Hooch was a gutsy dog, and no more so than when he had been at work. So I planned to put his food bowl in the kennel. We went to work and the next morning I put his food bowl in the kennel, sure enough, in he went and happily ate his dinner and looked at me. Laid on his bed and went to sleep. I went to bed leaving him there. No noise not a peep. He only made a noise when I woke up and had a look from the bedroom window. He clocked me straight away and started whining. I went downstairs to let him out and he came storming out and gave me a great welcome. I notched this one up as a success.

Had a great night at work, it's all going so well. I'm learning loads and loads. It's a proper joy, we always have fun and me and James are getting pretty close.

He seems to get me and understand if I'm a bit scared or confused. He only needs to point and I know which way we're going.

If I keep going like this, hopefully this will be my home for good. I get loads of exercise, loads of fun and the grub is good. I've never felt so good.

I guess probably the only downside is the kennel thing. I shouldn't have messed about yesterday but hey ho it's done now.

I wonder what we'll do today. In the back gate as normal, hope he's not going to try and get me in that kennel again. Ah look, there's dinner. All set out for me. Lovely.
The door has shut, I'm in my kennel, and I can't stop eating. Oh my god, it's like working with a bloody Jedi. Oh well, I'll sort it tomorrow. Sleep now I'm full. It's not a bad life huh!

Think Dog Think

So from then on he dined alfresco, in his kennel, he happily went in and learnt really quickly that when I woke up I would come and get him, he would run around in the garden until work time. It was a positive with his dinner to look forward too and lure him in, then a negative of having to stay in the kennel but then the positive was reinforced by the fun and antics when I woke up.

Any result that didn't involve conflict was great. Hooch could be really stubborn and in the next few weeks he showed me how stubborn he could be.

Things he learnt, he quickly unlearnt, then learnt again. He would attempt to fight me and challenge my dominance from time to time.

I had only had him for about three weeks and although he was an absolute joy to work with 90% of the time, the other 10% he was hard work. He would quite literally just dig his feet in, and although he was steadily losing weight he was still quite a lump to pull about. If he didn't want to go, we didn't go. He had to be coaxed or led gently sometimes, but the main thing I learnt was you had to win. If you didn't win, he would see it as a chance for a challenge and life would be hell again for a little while.

This "little while" could vary from an hour to days. You had to remain consistent and solid until he got over his little hissy fit. It was like being in charge of a moody toddler.

I had my hands full because he really could be amazing and then flip. The kennel was sorted and he seemed good with the arrangement there. No adjustments to that process. He was well behaved at home, played with the cat, got told off by the other dog.

Generally could be found sleeping in a door way or corridor making it difficult to get round him. He learnt so quick to be calm at home and everything was really tranquil.

The trick with association had really worked and he would get excited when he saw my uniform and get ready for the night ahead. It's a big obstacle, if your working dog doesn't like work, that's a head scratcher. Hooch had great nights, him and I would run about in the early hours play with a ball, mainly I was concentrating on tug at the moment.

I had booked up a training session with a friend of mine and I wanted Hooch to at least be able to bite on command and play a bit and let go when told. Just so I could show he was a good dog and in the space of a few weeks we were on it. I had high hopes for Hooch.

If you are going to do training and agility and obedience and make it enjoyable, you become of value to them.

Also the fact that you are leading them in these pursuits makes you leader by proxy. Always a good thing, and if it's done with reward motivation and not compulsion then it's even better for them.

As I say, with Hooch it was purely an exercise in fun and control. When walking around site as a dog handler it is imperative to look professional. As in most other professions the first impression can be the difference between a sale, a deal, a job.

Psychologically I believe if a criminal or trouble maker sees you heading towards them with a well trained dog in their mind they are already thinking this dog is well trained ergo capable.

A well trained dog is every criminal's worst nightmare. They can't outrun them, they can't hide and it takes a very brave person to fight a dog. Most people have an inbuilt fear including those who work with them.

Hooch had absolutely no malice in his day to day life, although at the time I thought he had it in him. It is important to remember you don't actually get bad animals. Some things they do are bad but it is all based on the situation.

I have had many conversations with many different people about the temperament of their dogs. The normal answer you get is, *"He wouldn't hurt a fly"*, or *"my dog wouldn't bite anybody."*

I am a dog lover, but would never trust a dog whole heartedly. Whether to bite or not is based solely on the situation. Not on the dog or his temperament.

It's not enough to say that he/she hasn't and you can never say he/she won't. As many people have explored in books and on television over the years a dog lives in the moment and one thing about nature is it will always find a way to defend itself. Every animal has an attack and defence. They will also use them when necessary with no remorse. We as humans aren't far from this. We can't say we wouldn't turn to violence, or we are pacifists. We just haven't been faced with that situation yet.

I couldn't be sure as we worked on a very relaxed site. As such we never came across situations that would cause him to become suspicious or aggressive.

Great for his agility and obedience training but nothing for his protection work. I knew from his looks not many people would take the chance that he wasn't trained. Most people looking at an eight stone dog would probably err on the side of caution.

So the plan was to go training, and to get him as far along as I could prior to taking him, he had a lot to live up too. I was really taken by him so the passion when I spoke about him came across as if I was 100% that Hooch would do it, but all dog handlers know. They aren't robots, and in the back of my mind was the couple of times he had met new people and his nerves had got the better of him.

He was getting much more self assured and seemed that people didn't bother him. His walk was and still remains amazing. He stalks like a lion, if he's approaching people or something he's not sure off, his head drops down and you can clearly see he is in hunting mode, the odd sniff of the air, the sheer focus and his gait becomes slow and assured. It's amazing to watch. When you call him at the park he comes back like the Littlest Hobo (showing my age) What I am trying to say is in the three or so weeks of having him he had really grown and become a self-assured dog, a bit more confidence. Confidence is so important.

All we had done had been for training and to build a bond but with this came confidence. Confidence in himself and also in me as his stability. Confidence for a dog is huge, it defines the dog. Also a lack of confidence will exhibit itself in so many ways and all will be counter productive, but I guess most importantly is the effect on its health.

Can you imagine being under stress day in day out, hour by hour and minute by minute. The effect this would have on your health would be huge, strained muscles, tiredness from concentration, not to mention all the unseen consequences.

Anything can trigger it. I've seen dogs scared of plastic bags. Toilet rolls, room lights being knocked, cars, fireworks, children, people. A dog only needs one bad experience and then that experience to be compounded by worriers. Humans have the same, we have irrational phobias, what could a moth do to me but I still feel edgy when they are about.

Phobias can be triggered from experience or suggestion but they all seem real, but we have a mind that thinks more deeply which can be a blessing or a curse. It can help us get a grip on it or if left unchecked the brain can catastrophise to a point of obsession and paranoia.

When I got Hooch, he had little experience in life and very little confidence due to his lack of exposure to anything, this was changing and you could see it. The big thing a dog cannot fake is its walk and its social standing. Other dogs know if your dog is faking it.

It is important that dogs, children, coworkers, anyone you come into contact with regularly must know boundaries. These boundaries give them the confidence to express themselves, speak candidly, and generally be themselves around you within these boundaries. They know how far they can go without upsetting, getting into trouble whatever it may be but it allows them the confidence to act freely within these boundaries.

It is why consistent managers get more honest and loyal staff. It is why a pack will follow a pack leader because pack leaders are consistent and not erratic. It is very difficult to work for or be friends with people who are erratic. It knocks your confidence because you never really know how your comments or actions are going to be received and so you constantly walk on egg shells.

So here is the contradiction that is confidence. You can not be good at you're job without confidence, you can be confident without being good at the job.

The point I am trying to make is that I have met plenty of people who have gone through life thinking they are ace and good at what they do because they have confidence.

Everyone around has known they aren't but they are happy and confident in their abilities.

This is a gift in itself, although somewhat annoying it is also infectious and can create some great results. *"Fake it until you make it"* is something many have done and done well.

I also have come across many people who are great at what they do yet don't believe it, and its crippling for them.

When you work a dog, confidence is the first thing you must get right, don't knock them too harshly, don't put too much pressure on them until they can handle it. That is, until they have the confidence to deal with it.

It is very similar to people. As I got the hang of dog handling and training I saw many people get a dog, walk onto a training field and put the dog under pressure to see if they could handle it!!

I wouldn't put my 12year old boy in the ring with a boxer without a bit of training and a pep talk. So there you have it, don't ask your dog to do anything you haven't prepared him for.

Don't have a dog unless you understand it isn't a democracy, its your way only. Sounds harsh and it can be, depends on the dog and how you've brought them up but I would be stressed if someone gave me a promotion to a role I couldn't handle.

That stress would possibly come out in a number of ways. None of them good for me or those around me. Sorry, this isn't a self help book, back to the story.

Hooch had taken to the tug, it was a mixed blessing. He would sit, he would bite the tug on command and let go.

All done in play drive, he loved it. He came in like he meant it and if you had the where with all to be looking at his tail, which was rare you would see it wagging like mad.

It was all fun and games. His front end meant it there was no doubt and his back end was happy as Larry. I was enjoying this because it was all my work, he was incredibly strong and his bite was accurate, powerful and always straight to the back of his mouth.

It was done with play drive. Because as I have explained the easiest way to make them understand is to do it with fun and play. It is no different to when you are asking your child to do something they don't want to do but when you make it fun they are all up for it.

I remember years ago I managed to get my children to wash my cars by making it fun. We used to always end up in a water fight and this was what the kids wanted to do. But they always started on the understanding that they had to wash the car. After one of them would get splashed a couple of times it would deteriorate into a water fight. It was fun and the kids washed the car. Baking, cooking, and tidying up, reading, homework. All learnt better with an edge of fun to them. Rarely worked out too well especially the baking but it was never dull and great memories were made.

There was always a time when these would become serious of course, but for now in the formative years let's just get them doing the activities. You can sharpen them up later.

Same in the dog training arena. To get your dog to recall you shout and whistle and make high pitched noises and even if the dog makes one step back in your direction you start cheering and congratulating. If they run past you go mad and it's all great you just want that one moment where they understand and then build on it. Many people think it's funny when I call Hooch even to this day because my voice is high pitched at first but if he ignores me my voice booms and as soon as he takes notice my voice goes high again.

For Hooch I would put the pressure on later. In the infamous words of Mick, *"the quickest way to train a dog is slowly"*

My dream was to take Hooch to become the great dog I believed he could be. I had already had so much feedback about him. All negative, if I'm honest it just spurred me on.

My plan was to train him to do events and really show partly that I could train a dog to a good standard but also to show all of the doubters that my cross breed could do it.

Hooch was a cross and a rescue with no history or pedigree. I knew he could do it though everyone seemed to doubt me. I truly believed that Hooch could compete and on an emotional level I was so in touch with him that I wanted him to fulfil his potential.

The dog world can be full of dog snobs. If you are going to work a dog it must be from working lines and especially from the lines that are in fashion at the time.

I would agree with some, there are certainly pedigrees that take less time and are more instinctive in what they do and I don't think anyone can doubt that. This happens in all lines, detection, protection any discipline.

People have this huge expectation of dogs, especially I find in pets.

A family or couple buy a dog, they read the books, internet. They find that this breed or that breed is perfect.

106

Good with kids, not too much exercise, minimum grooming, blah blah. Its like looking on Amazon. "Grooming , three stars out of five, do you want to read a customer review?"

The point is dogs are not made to measure, the breed doesn't mean it will be a cuddly lap dog. It's more likely to be, but its not a guarantee. You still have to do the training right, the socialisation. Or you might end up with a Shih Tzu that has a temperament like the Pit Bull's Amazon review.

Dogs aren't like buying a telly or a coffee maker. They aren't what the books say until you train them that way. I walk a lot with Hooch, less than I used to, I blame it on him and his age but I should look inward sometimes. However, I meet people with dogs all the time. *"Always had Labs, greatest dogs in the world. Always well behaved. Great with the kids.", "Always had Staffs, what an amazing dog. Never had an ounce of trouble with them."* In truth it wouldn't matter what dogs these people bought. Its the way they bring them up. Nothing more.

You do have breed specifics. 99% of collies will drive you mad with the amount of exercise they need. 99% of Spaniels are barmy. But the essence and personality, the tolerance levels, the eagerness to please, the appropriate behaviour, the calmness. That's 99% the owner and the environment they know to be theirs and calm and safe.

Many owners will buy dogs and allow them so much lea way. The lea way they give is because they have read the review and apparently this dog is a three star to train and a five start temperament.

It is important that your dog has rules and boundaries, not just for you and your chewable possesions and visitors hands, it's important for the dogs. If you give them too much room to move figuratively speaking, they have no idea where the boundaries are, and even worse when the boundaries keep moving.

Dogs need rules, the minute they get the whiff that they are choosing what they are doing they start believing they are in charge. This can be problematic in different ways for different dogs. None are good, you would never give your children more responsibity than they could handle. Not without consequences.

I have worked with guys who have paid a fortune because there dog is from the right region, country, and or lines. For sure these dogs take less training and cotton on so much quicker. But once the training is done it certainly doesn't mean they have seemed any better than a rescue dog from a pub in Four Marks or a stray white GSD.

The point I am trying to make is that once again you cannot take a dog from Belgium or a Czech GSD that are supposed to be the best lines or related to

107

world champions and just expect them to be good. Once again the review and the rating from the internet mean nothing. Once again we talk of the fact that people are buying dogs with a propensity to be good, to be able to achieve but this doesn't guarantee anything. You have to put the work in to ensure the dog uses the abilities they were born with. You have to train, you have to teach and most of all you have to nurture their natural abilities and whether their natural abilities would outstrip those of any other dog, you will never find out unless you nurture them well.

Hooch had abilities but he had a massive character too. Training was always fun and he always came across as an oaf, this wasn't helped by his huge belief in his ability to stop quicker than he could.

This is Hooch training to do a hold and bark but with way too much confidence in his ability to stop.

I remember talking to a gentleman who had allegedly been in the business for a long time and had a specific way of breeding his dogs to ensure the best dogs according to him. He said he could guarantee that all of the pups would become working dogs and be good working dogs. Unfortunately Mother Nature throws curve balls and nothing like this can be guaranteed. You can most definitely hedge your bets but that is as far as it goes. The rest is up to nature only.

The training with a tug proved it to me, he was a natural.

Sometimes it comes better when left to develop without training. Hooch had been 18 months with nobody pushing him to bite or putting him under pressure his bite had developed naturally into what dogs do naturally.

108

The idea that I had always had was reinforced by Hooch's willingness and quality of bite. It was about nurturing their nature not training. A dog will always fight like they mean it if they feel threatened, it is just their nature and instinct. If left alone to develop they will bite well and strong because no person has had any influence.

The minute you start training and not letting them just do what they do, as with anything. Human input can be the kill or cure.

Hooch was an absolute natural at biting so it was just about putting words to it.

Not every night but most nights I would do more with the tug as a game. I was slowly bringing it around to being more serious by fighting him more, not always letting him win. As I fought harder so did he, his snarling became throatier and he had an amazing drive to win, to be dominant. I knew I could use this. As the bite becomes strong and you reinforce that it is what you want from them the confidence grows and you can watch their body language change and become more dominant. The chest puffs out and the head stays high. They can't hide their emotions and they have to go through the posturing because it is ingrained. You can watch this as you train. This is what was happening to Hooch, he was going through the motions, so I started pushing him with my knees, covering his eyes. Just putting gentle pressure on. Never hurting him but just making him feel uncomfortable.

You can try this out with a simple exercise. If you take your dog for a walk, start marching, walk with a purpose, with a destination. Watch your dog's chest puff out and their walk becomes more assured. This is because the walk becomes all that is going through their mind and with their leader the confidence grows.

So I took him to Mick's. I had high hopes but Hooch hadn't done this with anybody else around, and in the back of my mind were his few meetings with strangers that hadn't gone well.

We used to train in a farmer's field over by Malden Rushett. It was a great spot and Mick was a great trainer. He had many answers and seemed to be able to get into the heads of dogs and work solutions out that I rarely understood until he explained.

I pulled up and got out of my car. There was Mick busying himself around his van. I had a chat with him; he wanted to know about Polar and what had happened.

Mick collected a wealth of knowledge about dogs so was always interested in anything that your dog had done, hadn't done. Illnesses, nutrition and all sorts. The great thing was, Mick would use it for the good of all the other people he trained. He had a very matter of fact way of explaining things. It worked well for me and I learnt a lot.

So I stood chatting for a bit, it didn't matter with Mick you could get just as much training and learning with your dog in the cage as you did with him out, but after a chat Mick said *"come on then, let's see him"*

So out came Hooch, his first appearance. I was getting nervous now. Mick would tell you the truth and so here was Hooch's time to shine.

I walked over to Mick with him. *"Great, look at him. What did you say he was?"* He looked distraught. Mick was in his late 50's maybe 60. He was not very tall and Hooch was probably as big as him. *" He's a GSD x Rotti"*, Mick looked at me and just said. *"Why, why did you get him, he's too big to have any stamina, and he'll be slow."*

It was time for me to try and get Mick to understand why I had brought him. Usually you would bond for longer before looking at bite work, also Hooch wasn't very fit, and he was still a good 10 kgs overweight. But I had faith, this was it *"I just want to know, if he will or he won't"* Meaning protect me, as much as you want all the other disciplines, you need to know your dog will protect you. Mick looked sceptical but as always he would do his best to try and get him right for working. If he couldn't he would tell me.

"Alright come on then, has he bitten a sleeve?" He hadn't, he had been on the tug but that was it, also he hadn't bitten with anyone else around. *"We'll start at the top then, I'm going to stand over there by that bush and you send him in off lead, let's see if he even has a clue. We'll know where to start with him."*

So there I am in a cold field about 20 foot away from Mick, Hooch seems interested which is a good sign, Mick starts becoming animated waving the protective sleeve about. Hooch was really on it. I was holding Hooch at the collar and he started bouncing on his back feet.

This is great, this is the kind of intensity you want. He was chomping at the bit. If I can just pause time.

It's really important now to seize the day. When a dog is interested it's so important to time it right. So as always Mick waves the sleeve to say he's ready. From then on it's up to the handler when the you let go of the dog. The baiter is ready, but it's always best to let go when the dog is excited and at the top of his excitement, and also when he's bouncing forward if you can so he can move with his motivation.

This is important as I have seen many dogs let go at the wrong time, when they are on the back foot. This is bad, the dog tends to be surprised and you lose milliseconds, if you're after someone or you want the run and bite to look impressive you go with the momentum of the dog.

Hooch was really bouncing forward trying to break from me, his head kept turning to look at me trying to get me to let go. He looked really excited, no aggression just an instinct to do what he felt he needed to do. His eyes were alight and intense. He was such a natural at this, there was no straining against the lead just a gentle pressure showing me he wanted to go forward. Always forward.

As Hooch surged forward, I let go. He went screaming off to get Mick, he always acted surprised when he launched and his body would bunch up as he lowered his body and surged forward with his powerful back legs. He wasn't quick but he went forward with an assuredness that he had learnt from the confidence I had begun to instil in him. I could only imagine what he was processing. Hooch has complete tunnel vision in these moments and it was all about Mick right now. I could imagine his target filling his entire vision.

He hit Mick with a crash, Mick caught him on the sleeve perfectly but couldn't hold up to the impact went backwards into the bush. I called for Hooch to "*OUT*" and called him back. Back came Hooch with his best Littlest Hobo trot and came to a heel next to me. I told him "*down*" which he did. All good so far. I trotted over to Mick. "*You Ok mate?*" His reply was the best I could have wished for, "*you know what*" he said, "*he f****** will.*"

I don't want to overstate this, but the point I am trying to make is worth overstating. George wouldn't bite. I knew this even with my inexperience I knew this.

Max would bite because someone else trained him and trained him well.

Polar would bite because it was an instinct born of fear and nervousness.

But I had trained Hooch. By nurturing his natural instincts he had shone. He had never done this before I taught him the command to go in and the command to go out. He protected me and he done it amazingly. I don't know how to explain the feeling of elation I felt when this happened.

You see Hooch was my work, I know he was doing what his instincts told him. But his confidence and his assertiveness were my training. On my own, it's difficult to explain the feeling. It is one of pride in Hooch and myself.

Like when your son or daughter scores their first goal, or wins their first race and that smile breaks from your lips that show nothing but pride. The feeling that you knew they could do it but nobody else did. Because you helped and you believed and you supported.

There is a similar pride with your dog when you ask them to protect you and with no question or hesitation they just get to it.

It is a feeling of power to and I'm not ashamed of that. I went to work on a daily basis, hoping for no trouble but always wanting the confidence that if there was he had my back. And here we were, and he had.

There was no ambiguity or hesitation. He had hit Mick with an almighty force, no stutter just straight through.

More than that, when I told him to OUT he dropped off with no residue malevolence. Just a job well done. He then swung back round when I brought him to heel, ready for round two. That's my boy.

HAHA, call me fat would you?? Question my breeding?? Well that showed you little sod.

What a rush. That was great, I feel invigorated. I took that little bloke straight into the bush. He won't be slating me again. I've just fallen on my feet with James and he thinks he can come along talking like he knows me. Ha

Oops, James is calling. Best go back to him. I can show him I am a good lad and hopefully he won't get angry. I think that's what he wanted me to do. Me and him have been doing this on a tug and I've quite got the hang of it I think.

Oh yeah, James is smiling like a cat that got the cream. That was definitely what he wanted and by god it was what I wanted to do. I hope I get to do it again to that bloke. I never get angry, see what you did.

Lay down, yes James of course. Oh yeah I'm feeling it now. I'm not really built for speed.

Honestly I would have been chuffed with a lesser result but this was awesome and I knew then that he was going to be a cracker. He was only a month or so into his training and he already showed his confidence.

He did another bite and Mick let him win the sleeve.

This means that Mick let go of the sleeve and allowed Hooch to run off with it. This gives Hooch the chance to parade his trophy, and it is a trophy. He won that with his strength and confidence.

This is another show of how sensitive dogs are to signs given off by us. When you let them win the sleeve you then parade them around so they can puff out their chest and swagger. Let them revel in the moment while you tell them how good they are. Hooch always heeled on the left so when you parade them you run anti clockwise in a circle. This way you are always on the outside which means you are herding them and showing them the way to go.

Even in victory you must give them the impression you are in charge.

This is the great conundrum in dog handling.

I talk to people about pack leaders and alpha dogs reasonably regularly. When you are walking your dog or feeding him etc, the popular opinion is that you should always remain at the head of the pack. This is widely known and works, as long as you do it with respect and assertion. Not aggression.

The difficulty in dog handling is you have to hand over the reins to your dog in some situations the dog takes control of the situation. You can hold on to the lead but really the dog is all over it.

He is open to a couple of important commands but that is only because the pattern is to bite then OUT, so the dog is waiting for the OUT cue. Apart from that the dog is in the zone and controlling the situation. This is all assuming your dog is balanced and confident. Otherwise he would be tearing at the sleeve like a crazy dog or cowering away.

Your job is to get your dog OUT when he has finished his job. That truly is it.

You are monitoring because you need to know your dog is doing it right and not inflicting any more pain than it needs to, or losing control and just as important is your dog's comfort in the bite.

You get dogs that do what some people call a typewriter bite. This is when the dog goes up and down the arm releasing and re-biting. You can't have this. The idea of the dog is to bite and hold. It isn't about damaging people, tearing arms off. It is all about control, firstly it is about deterrent but if it comes to it you want and need your dog to bite and hold until told to release.

What I mean about comfort for the dog is, as I said earlier the best bites are to the back of the mouth, clamp down and hold. No ragging, no typewriter just hold. This shows the dog has confidence in its ability, that it has been taught to bite properly, and as a bi-product it hasn't hurt itself in the bite which does happen.

The process of handing over control sounds hard doesn't it. To remain in control while allowing the dog to think he's in control. But in that second you then need to regain control with your voice and back to pack leader.

It isn't as hard as it seems and for some they don't even notice they do it. If you have had children you've done this.

You know when you tell your child that he/she is better than you at something, doesn't matter if it's true or not. But you hand the reins over in that moment. You tell the child to take control. As a parent you do this because one day you want them to take control and let you have a spare room.

But this is how we prepare our children for the big wide world. *"Course you can, you're better at it than me"*, *"well done, I would never have got to grips with that computer"* it's all making your children believe in themselves, and learning that sometimes they are going to have to take control because they are good at what they do or because they have no choice but to get on with it. By handing over the reins from time to time and giving responsibility to them it teaches them to have confidence in their own abilities.

We do it at work, sometimes you will ask questions to someone that you know is good at that area. This is all the same thing. You make them feel empowered. It

114

doesn't have to be true. You don't even need the answer but that two minute chat can fill someone with confidence or just massage their ego. It all goes back to what I was saying earlier. It depends on what that person values.

The problem is not enough people seem to do it anymore.

Parents seem to want to do everything for their children to show what amazing parents they are or possibly because it's just easier to do it themselves.

This compromises the child in my opinion. Its why so many kids are leaving home and instantly ballooning because they have no idea how to cook or what to cook.

That's if they didn't balloon before they left home because they did nothing to help in the house because they were too busy dodging the sun and playing on games consoles.

Why would you ask your child to go out in the world without preparing them for what's out there and the things that they need to think about. There is so much but we can help. As parents we can help and explain. But by the time they are looking to move out we can really only guide and nurture because very similar to dogs, kids have a push pull reflex too. If you tell them what they should do I guarantee you'll get nowhere but if you explain, lay out the consequences of their actions and let them make the decision. Then at least you can inwardly chuckle when they ignore your words and go and do what you said wouldn't work and it didn't.

I'm digressing again.

I believe it is hugely important to hand over control and responsibility gently to children as they grow up and it's just as important in dogs.

This also includes scent work, indication for dogs obviously. You hand control over but need to be confident you can regain it immediately. This can work for you as well. Dogs aren't dissimilar to people in that if you put your faith in people they will generally see that as a compliment and rise to the challenge.

Generally, with dogs it's similar.

I used to follow Hooch if he picked up a scent because I wanted him to know I trusted him and his skills. Again, they don't think like that but it does work.

When you put your faith in them, when Hooch's nose hit the floor sniffing and I slackened the lead and began to walk behind him instead of next to him he instinctively took up the scent and started moving with more urgency.

Now if I had reined him back in every time he noticed a fresh smell, how many times before he gives up trying to show me whatever he is trying to show me.

But when Hooch put his nose down with that urgent sniffing he did, I would say *"find it"* with comparative urgency to push him on so he would know I was watching him and knew what he wanted to do.

It only took a couple of times and he knew, he knew where to be. He knew I would drop in behind him. He knew my pace would rise with his. It is a lovely thing to watch if you have ever thought of doing training with a dog I don't think you can go wrong with scent work. It stimulates them and makes you work together which can only be great for your bond.

But this is how the balance has to work when you are working a dog, and it becomes very complicated and can become confused if you let it. But again, make it simple. Don't put caveats on it. You are pack leader; he is working for you and some things he is allowed to take ownership. Simple.

Same as in the work place. How many businesses don't grow because the owner won't allow anybody else to hold the reins?

Or in extreme cases won't even take extra staff on because it would in their minds compromise the quality that their customers expect.

Though this is a noble quest and if you are happy doing 16 hour days and answering the phone all the time because you won't accept that there may be someone out there who is as keen to find and employer who will put their faith in them as you are trying to find someone to put your faith in.

You have to take the leap sometimes. To do nothing is to fail, so try. Take someone on, give someone responsibility.

Hand the reins over a bit at a time and you may be surprised.

I could not tell you how many small business's I have spoken to and will never get any bigger due to the fact the owner just will not delegate.

I get it, many small business owners have put their heart and soul into their business and much of the business has their personality running all the way through it and their customers expect to be dealt with in that way and the product to be delivered with the love and quality that they are used to.

The beauty of us humans and dogs too is that we are very good at mimicking. Also mimicking is hard wired into us, subconsciously we cannot help it. We gravitate to people we would like to emulate or aspire to.

It is a well-known fact in body language circles that we do this subconsciously. We copy the leader of the group or the person we aspire to.

This doesn't mean the loudest or most rambunctious. This means the person that our instincts draw us to as a leader.

We have used this trait to train our working dogs for many years. But we can use this to teach our new staff as long as you are pack leader and someone to emulate, then your new staff will do exactly that and they will try to mimic you and your qualities and also the desire to keep the companies name and reputation.

So Hooch's training had started. Mick and I continued to train with Hooch whenever I got the chance, I remember Mick had a dog called Ike, and if I remember rightly he was a GSD x Belgian Malinois.

Ike was quite a piece of kit, he was sharp, quick, obedient and most of all he was intimidating. The first time I took a bite from him I remember thinking, "*I hope Hooch looks like this to the baiters.*"

When we were training, Mick sent Ike in to do a hold and bark, a hold and bark is when the dog runs from the handler at the baiter on a command, gets close up to the baiter but doesn't bite. Instead he/she barks and intimidates. This is for when you want to stop someone but don't want the dog to bite.

The idea is to hold the criminal in place. The handler shouts his challenge, something like "*don't move, my dog is trained to bite*" or something as politically correct as you can come up with but with a little bit of threat thrown in for effect. If the criminal moves the dog goes in for the bite.

I wanted to do some training with Hooch to get him to do his bark and hold. Ike was just showing me the standard to which I was to aspire to.

I was stood in the middle of the field we trained in. Mick issued his challenge and I stood perfectly still. Ike came storming in.

He had such a turn of speed he was on you before you knew it. I stood and something about Ike made you look into his eyes. But there was something in his eyes that meant you couldn't look away. It was malevolence, a feeling that all he wanted you to do was move so he could nail you.

There was an evil in that dog when he was challenging you and it was all consuming. I was looking into his eyes, and I had frozen, Mick was shouting at me to move so Ike could bite but I was rooted, I don't know what it was, I think I even stopped breathing for those moments. I had to force myself to move, it's so counter intuitive anyway. I mean, if someone says to you "*move so my dog can bite you*" in your mind you're thinking, "*well I won't move then!!*" but there was something about Ike that even with a sleeve and knowing he was arm true I still couldn't.

I had never had that feeling of fear before or after with any dog I have baited. Ike was a one off.

Later I was talking to Mick about it and Mick said he had the same problem when competing. The baiter was supposed to move to allow the dog to bite but many lost their bottle. Glad I wasn't the only one. Mick put it down to this; Ike stared at you dead in the eye. Not many dogs did. Mick had trained him to do so.

I wanted this, Hooch was a great biter, the power was quite epic and because a lot of the tug work I had done with him I had allowed Hooch to run through. Holding the tug to the side of me. Hooch would grab the tug on the way through and keep running. This taught Hooch to bite and keep running, so when he bit he kept powering through which in turn took many baiters of their feet.

It actually did more than this as a friend of mine Ryan Murphy found out.

Hooch had an amazing skill of bringing his feet up to hit you in the gentleman's parts as he came in. He did it to everyone. So much so that anyone who has ever baited Hooch knows to turn at a sideways angle. I forgot to mention this to Ryan but that's another story.

This picture demonstrates, he used to come in hard and fast but his first foot would hit home and then he would place the second foot using it to push back on.

Now we had perfected his bite and I didn't want to do too much on the bite. The old adage *"if it isn't broke, don't fix it."*

So I concentrated on changing things around. Hold and bark, emergency stops. If you can make their training nice and routine at the beginning it works wonders. Remember I said routine and consistency. This is all good if you want a show dog, or an obedience champion.

The issue with this when you are working a dog is that you have no idea what is going to happen next. You don't want your dog to pre empt you because you may need him to hang on to that arm for longer or shorter or not bite at all. You cannot pre plan.

So the way to beat this is to change what he does and change it regularly. Get their training right and get them to the standard you want. Then start changing things.

They must react to you and the only way to prove this to yourself is to change things and get them to react to your voice. The more you do it the more they will listen. If they wander around like a clockwork robot around a 5, 10 or 100 acre site it makes no difference. They will always act like a clockwork robot.

The dog must understand that at any minute everything could change and they have to react to what you charge them to do.

There is an important distinction. I never did this at home.

Home was to relax, but at work I watched as dog handler after dog handler would walk around sites the same way and stop in the same places for their dog to wee and you could see they were both mentally asleep.

Pet owners do it now when I'm out with Hooch, on their phones or listening to music. The dog knows you aren't in the slightest bit interested in them and off they go. You wonder now why your dog was so badly behaved at the park. Why don't you pick your head up, stop looking at social media on your phone and give your dog some attention.

They want to please you, but you have to give them the chance and if they can't reach you through your addiction to constant communication or social media then just like children they will look for any attention they can get. Even if it's bad.

It really is just like children. I am going to rant for a second. I watch young parents taking their kids to school ignoring their children and it's the same epidemic, I see tables of people looking at their phones instead of interacting. I talk to the tops of my children's heads because they are looking at their phones.

Dogs and children need attention. It is up to you how much you give them but you will rue the day when you look up from your phone and they have grown up and you missed teaching them those lessons because you were too busy looking at how lovely next doors morning walk was with the dog or what your mates Sunday dinner looked like.

If I could teach everyone one thing from this book it would be to instead of looking at pictures of sunsets or woodland walks or bands that people went to see. Go and do it. Put your phone down and enjoy the outdoors with your dog or with your children and actually be there with them. Not just in the vicinity.

I am lucky enough to remember a time when my parents took us on holiday we had them there, when I go and see them now. They are in the room, literally and metaphorically. There is no greater gift you can give to your child or your dog than be with them actually be with them.

This is how you train dogs and dare I say it train children. Be with them, give them your attention and they will look for these good attentions, and they will produce good behaviour to obtain these rewards of your time and attention.

So back to the training, I was trying to train him the hold and bark, he had a lazy bark. Trust me, it was good enough to make sure most people didn't move, but I wanted more. He wasn't quick like Ike, he didn't surprise you with his speed.

You always have to work to strengths. Hooch was never going to be quick like Ike. So you play to their strengths. Hooch's strength was his strength. He was about 52kgs now and you could see he was a powerful dog, when he barked he showed all of his 42 teeth and he had a big mouth. But all of this was a game to him, he enjoyed it and as such didn't have that aggressive bark. Upon releasing him for the bite in training he would run at the baiter like a sidewinder missile. He never stayed in the centre like most dogs he weaved side to side. His running was odd, some people would say that if a dog attacks from the side it is weak in confidence so it won't attack straight preferring a sneaky attack. Hooch didn't come from the side but the way he ran he was always off centre. It was a bit of a nightmare for the baiter. Catching a dog safely and not getting hurt or hurting the dog were primary for them. Running in a straight line aided this but to this day Hooch seems incapable of running a straight line even when playing.

I spoke to Mick about why Hooch didn't have a particularly aggressive bark. Mick was convinced that it was much more to do with his size than anything else. You tend to find with smaller dogs with loads of energy their bark is sharp, high pitch and quick. The bigger the dogs the slower and lower tones of the bark making it sound less urgent for want of a better word. Some of this is purely biological. The bigger the chest the deeper the bark. But you could do things to make it sound more aggressive and make it quicker and more urgent.

120

Dogs have several different drives, each drive comes into play dependant on the situation. If a dog is under threat they tend to be in defence. The popular belief is that in defence dogs attack out of fear, because of the pressure they are under, pressure they have not been taught to cope with.

This leads to fear biters. But they exude aggression. Also dogs learn little or nothing in when in defence because they are in survival mode and like humans react with their reptilian brain as it's called or fight and flight reaction. This survival instinct is deep rooted and bypasses the rational brain.

In humans this has huge physical reactions, blood leaves the extremities and makes its way to the major organs, adrenalin is released, and hairs rise from the body to make us look bigger from a time when we were hairy.

It is even believed that urinating and defecating is to make us lighter to run away. It's that deep rooted. It is the same in dogs, and to make your dog deal with these situations you have to instil massive amounts of confidence.

Hooch oozed confidence on the training field. After only a month or two of training, he had grown into a dog that believed he couldn't lose. He had a couple of hang ups which will become clear later but in the main and on the training field with Mick and I he had never lost a fight. He hadn't undergone any pressure; nobody had pushed him backwards as they call it.

So Hooch was King Kong, in his mind. When he went in for the bite, he had no idea it might go wrong, it didn't even enter his head. So on the hold and bark he was lazy, it was a complacency that he had.

So Mick and I went to work. I had a conversation with Mick that will never leave me. About four training sessions after he met him Mick asked me to put Hooch away in the car after we had been doing some training. I did and then wandered back to Mick to listen to the summary of our session.

Great, that little fella has asked James to put me away. Here goes, he's going to slate me again isn't he.

Wait until I get out and get to do another bite. I'll flatten him.

Although, training has been going really well. Mick I think is his name, he seems to be pretty cool with me now. I wonder if he's complimenting my work.

I've been doing some finding stuff, some walking in squares, having a lay down and a sit down. It's been pretty good.

Maybe I've won him over with my devilish charm. I guess we will wait and see. I'm going to have a snooze.

Are there any hot dogs left?

121

Mick's training style and his communication suited me down to the ground. He was blunt and critical but always with a solution, at least a potential solution.

He was a glass half full kind of guy. I had pretty much stopped going to M by now because I had learnt what I needed to from them and now needed one on one to develop further.

M had been amazing for me as a beginner but I needed more than group training now, especially with Hooch and how far I wanted to go with him.

Together you and I shall experience a bond only others like us will understand.

When outsiders see us together their envy will be measured by their disdain.

I was at Mick's and he wanted to have a word about Hooch. I always listened to Mick's opinion and tried to act upon it.

Mick had been completely taken by Hooch also. He told me in this conversation that I could do anything I wanted with Hooch, he was a special dog. Attentive, loyal and very trainable. He also had such a bond with me that training was quite easy. As long as I was with him and he had me as a crutch Hooch would go anywhere and do anything. He had a keen mind and took to training effortlessly.

It was a slightly different conversation to our first one about Hooch.

Hooch had come on leaps and bounds and was showing me very quickly that the potential I had seen in him on our first meeting was right. His energy was great and by the power of association he had learnt where and when he could use his energy.

The energy level when you did training was amazing for a big dog. If anything I had to bring his energy down to focus him in training. On the training field he was alert, upbeat and clearly enjoying himself. When doing obedience his whole posture would change and he would walk around proudly doing as was asked of him.

I couldn't have been prouder, after all the negative press I had received about Hooch, his breeding, his size, his stamina. To get this sort of feedback, I could feel my chest swell.

It is very similar to any breakthrough where you have put time and effort into something but with dogs as with children and friends or people you are training. You give a part of you to the training and Hooch had most certainly become a large part of my life. To think that I had come from knowing very little to getting to a point with a dog where he was a product of my training and time was a great feeling. Made only better as I knew what a sheltered life he had come from.

Hooch was a dream at home now; he had lost about 10kgs so was looking trim and powerful. He still couldn't run fast or do agility particularly well but his sheer bulk made up for all of this. Mick's closing comment was "*there is nothing this dog won't do for you*".

This kind of statement doesn't come easy from Mick's lips so I took as a kind of trophy. It had been a short but tiresome journey so far but knowing you were on the right track meant that I could carry on in the direction I was going knowing it was working. Just like a dog it gave me the confidence to keep stepping forward.

123

So I left the training ground delighted. I couldn't wait to get on the phone to my friends Phil and Keith. It had been a hard slog for two months. Hooch had tried my patience more than any dog I had dealt with. Stubborn, hard to train and erratic.

But it had all come to this point where I was so proud of him. On the training field he didn't miss a beat. He hit hard every time. He looked to the man not the sleeve, which is good. Some dogs I knew would only attack if the baiter had a sleeve on but we had worked hard not to make Hooch sleeve obsessed and he wasn't.

As much training was done when Hooch had to walk across the sleeve to bark at the baiter with no sleeve on just to make sure the sleeve wasn't his focus point. Many working dogs will only attack or bark up if the baiter had a sleeve on. This is obviously no good in real situations because very few burglars wear anything that resembles a sleeve.

His obedience was coming on so well and he was really looking to me for direction and confidence. It was exactly what I wanted out of a dog.

At home he was the best friend you could ask for. He followed me around and wanted attention from time to time. He stayed within view of me on walks and had become a true companion. There were very few places I couldn't take him because he was so well behaved and calm. Everywhere we went he was commented on and met people with no nervousness at all now.

Every now and then he would challenge me and become obstinate for a day or two. This I expected, he was a very dominant dog and was just pushing the boundaries to see if he could challenge my leadership. I just remained consistent, did a bit of extra training and didn't let it frustrate me. I knew the end result would be worth the time and effort.

I came to enjoy a challenging dog, I find them interesting and like many things in life it would be boring without a bit of challenge. I see many dogs when out walking and I have a fondness for the naughty ones, the mischievous type and I know many get out of hand and that's where the fun stops. They do need boundaries but they need fun too. You can have the best behaved dog in the world but when I look in their eye and there is no fire, just a vacant stare they have been pushed too hard. Dogs should be allowed to be dogs. Some things can't be excused but you should allow them to have fun just like children. Without this they forget the meaning of their existence and just become robots that walk next to you around a square park once in the morning once in the evening never deviating from their pattern. This isn't what a dog is meant to do. It wasn't what I wanted Hooch to do or any other dog I have in the future. Hooch's challenging behaviour became a joke around the house and it was met with consistency and calmness. He wasn't allowed of lead if he pulled his way to the park. He would only get let off if he walked nicely. Reward and motivation.

I went to training more and more, my fixation for his training was built on his success and how much further I believed I could take him. It became important for me to show what I could do as a trainer and handler.

He was the first dog that would be my work and though I was getting guidance the work and the time was mine. The training and the work had become a huge part of my life and as such my home life was really struggling. Sadly without me really noticing.

I was spending so much time away or asleep or training. All with the best intentions, I wanted to build a great reputation as a trainer and handler. I was always in work, I was reliable and conscientious because I loved the job and I was enjoying my work and training so much. It was difficult to say if this was a symptom of my home life or the home life was a symptom of all my working.

I had now met a few people from different training clubs and whilst working that I had quite a circle of associates and went to different training sessions in different places to really learn more theories and see how they worked with different dogs.

Every night I went to work and it was me and Hooch just doing our thing, no pressure apart from the odd incident. It suited me so well.

It didn't suit my wife. I was doing it for us as a family and my plan was to build a great business for the future, for our family. But like many misguided souls trying to do the right thing, it wasn't received as I thought it would be.

My wife and I decided to break up again. It was the right thing, we weren't getting on and I was working as hard as I could to keep the family going, I didn't want to live in poverty or struggle. I wanted to have a comfortable life and to do that, I had to work hard. My then wife didn't get it, she wanted me at home.

The main problem was that we had grown up in different worlds, my world was work hard to get what you want and rest later on in life, her world was salaried and Monday to Friday going out for lunch and drinks with like-minded people.

My life was hairy arsed dog handlers and hourly pay. Keeping the wolf from the door by working a lot of hours.

So we decided to go our separate ways.

For a while I was a bit manic and run down. It's hard to explain the strength I took from Hooch. He had remained consistent in my life and was always happy to see me. My dad imparted some wisdom in his usual dry way, my mum and dad never understood fully why I had come from gainful steady employment to become a dog handler. They understood my love of animals, but they weren't into dogs. My dad has a healthy respect of dogs; my mum is a bit scared of them.

When my Mum first met Hooch I had been working in Birmingham at festival for a few nights and I decided to drop in to see my Mum and Dad for the night. I had been working hard and was pretty tired. It was a lovely day and I pulled up on the drive of their house. I left Hooch in the car knowing that Hooch was going to have to stay on lead while I was there.

I was really confident with Hooch and how well behaved he was. But as I have said he was quite a size and I knew this would make my Mum uneasy. I went in for a cuppa. Hooch could rest in the car for a bit. I was chatting to my parents in the garden when my Dad said, *"you might as well bring him through. Just keep him on his lead."* I went and got him.

I walked him round into the garden and I knew from my Mums face he made my Mum slightly uneasy. Hooch's greatest quality is his calmness and walking around the garden with his slow measured gait he really showed this.

Mum was ok with dogs as long as they left her alone. Mum could be in the vicinity as long as they were calm and didn't want any attention from her. This usually worked as dogs have a sixth sense. If you're not interested in them they are rarely interested in you. Hooch came and sat next to me at the table. He was really well behaved and I guess maybe after working a couple of nights he didn't fancy being lively anyway.

As time went on Mum could see he was quite happy laid there. Mum said *"you can take him off his lead if you want. I just don't want him to close to me."* This I did and every time Hooch moved towards my Mum I just called him back. Everyone was happy.

Dad was quite entranced by him and I think from the outset Dad rather liked him and nothing has really changed there.

My Dad has always explained it away by saying that Hooch has a kind face. But I actually think it goes deeper than this. It is similar to when people of spiritual persuasion talk about aura. Hooch has calmness and I think it surrounds him. It seems to engulf those around him.

I know many people and many organisations that claim this about all dogs. I agree many do, but I believe this to be mainly due to the relationship and value that the individual puts on the dog. I know my daughter for example will stop mid-sentence to go and meet a dog and as for dog shows I spend more of my time looking for her than looking at dogs. She has been no different from a young child and I truly believe for her there is a connection and a calmness to be had due to her relationship with dogs.

Hooch seems to have this talent whether you find this quality in dogs or not.

Hooch won everyone over and by the end of my visit he was wandering around off lead and both Mum and Dad were quite comfortable with him. He had the run of the house except for the kitchen.

He was supposed to sleep in the porch that night. My parents didn't want to be tripping over him in the night.

I put him away and said goodnight, I was just dozing off when I heard Hooch running up the stairs. I opened the bedroom door and there he was with his best PDSA face on. He stared at me imploringly and I just wheeled him round and took him back downstairs. He didn't struggle or object he just wandered back into the porch and turned back around to face me with his sad eyes. I talked to him for a moment. You may laugh but I know I'm not the only one. I spoke to him about staying where he was and I would see him in the morning.

I went back to bed and no sooner had I got in bed but Hooch was coming up the stairs again. That's why he didn't object because he knew he could just come straight back up again. I didn't want to make a big thing of it so I settled him down in my room and decided to explain to my parents the next day.

I woke up in the morning. Hooch had been great and just gone straight to sleep. I took him downstairs. My parents were in their usual spot with tea and looked at me quizzically as Hooch entered the room behind me.

I explained what had happened. Upon closer inspection Hooch had used his teeth on the brand new PVC door handle to turn it and pull it towards him to get out. He had made a little bit of a mess of the handle.

He was a sneak and for all his macho traits and size he will not sleep in a room without somebody. Because of mine and his bond he would prefer it to be me but anyone will do in my place. But never on his own.

A very good friend of mine Ryan Murphy and his family look after Hooch if I am away. It doesn't happen often and I know Ryan's family look forward to his visits so I know he gets looked after.

He stayed there the first time and come bed time he went in the kitchen with the other dogs. Ryan had a couple of dogs one was Hooch's age and one was young.

So as he did with his other dogs Ryan left them in the kitchen and closed the door. He got in bed with his wife and before he knew it his wife was waking him telling him someone was wandering around downstairs.

Of course Ryan found Hooch milling around downstairs trying to find his humans I expect. Ryan put him back and went to bed. Hooch broke back out again very soon and Ryan found him squeaking at the bottom of the stairs. Hooch has a very annoying squeak that he never seems to get bored of doing if he is stressed or excited. It can go on for a long time and is so hard to ignore.

In the end Ryan put him back in the kitchen and sat on the stairs waiting to see how he did it. Sure enough Hooch used his mouth to turn the handle and out he walked again. Ryan spent three nights on his couch in the front room so Hooch would sleep and brings it up in conversation often. Hooch really doesn't like sleeping on his own.

This is Hooch with Ryan's young dog Marley. He's exceptionally tolerant.

When I left my ex-wife I drove straight up to my parents. It's funny how it doesn't matter how old I get I think they are still my first port of call.

They were having some time on their boat on the river. I rung and told Dad what had happened and Dad said without hesitation, "*If Hooch is ok on the boat just come straight up. Stay for a few days*." I took Hooch and went.

It was a lovely few days. There is something very calming about being on the river. Just bobbing about with a beer in your hand. Nature all around and the weather was kind to us. We chatted and had a good laugh and a few beers sat on river banks and in pubs. Had breakfast on the barbecue.

We had met them on the boat in a small village called Littleport. I didn't know how Hooch would take this; it's not a dog's natural environment on a boat.

Hooch loved it, from the moment we pulled up and I got him out of the car, he was running around on the bank, I got on the boat and he just jumped on.

When we were chugging along the river, Hooch could be found just sitting looking out over the river. It was like he was having a break too.

We were moored in Littleport and we went to a little country pub that evening the name eludes me.

I was sat talking about the situation and what I was going to do and explaining the main reason for the split was the dogs.

It was definitely an *"it's me or the dog"* moment when we split. Dad said to me, *"I never understood why you got into working with dogs"*, I was going to try and explain but then he said *"I think I get it now, Hooch always wags his tail when he sees you, and your missus doesn't"*

That one sentence sums up my entire situation. My ex-wife was giving me a hard time for what I thought I was doing right, Hooch never judged, got the hump, he never put demands on me.

It sounds strange to say but, after a year of falling in and out with her it was obvious we would never share my passion for dogs, and although she loved dogs and enjoyed having one as a pet it wasn't the same.

I really could see my future would always be working with them or being around them. This was never going to butter any parsnips for her and over the

130

last couple of year's dogs had become hugely important in my life and I hope I don't sound like a crazy dog person but I am unashamed about this.

Hooch and his success had become a large part of my life. It started moulding my identity. The enjoyment of training was only enhanced by his willingness to train and if people forgot my name or didn't know I was now *"that bloke with Hooch"*

To this day I swear there are people that wouldn't recognise me without Hooch.

I moved into a flat temporarily and then to a mobile home on a caravan park to keep cost down. As much as this was an awful time for me, it also allowed me to get on with what I wanted to do.

I was still working at the Russians house; I worked 13 out of 14 nights and had one off to see my children. They would all bundle round and sleep in the mobile home. It was like a holiday for them and after all of the tension and hardships of the last few months it was like a holiday for me too.

The kids and I had a great time and I have many happy memories from this time in my life. I had a lovely garden which in the summer the kids and I were always in. We planted sunflowers and had sunflower races. I won these; I mowed the kid's ones by accident.

We were always doing stuff and there was always a feeling of calm around the place.

Considering it was a difficult time we made the best of it and though my children lived a long way away we always made what little time we had together count.

Hooch and I also built an even stronger bond, it truly was just me and him against the world a lot of the time. Hooch took this very seriously and rarely left me alone. Wherever I was, he was too. Any walks or trips he had to come because I had nobody to look after him.

I'm not quite sure what's going on. James and I have up sticks and moved to a caravan. I thought caravans were for holidays and this is becoming a very long holiday. It's just me and him all the time now except for every now and then the little people pop over.

My god, you have no idea how annoying they are. One of them sleeps in my bed, would you believe it. I have to get in bed with the bigger one. But then she gets really hot and I don't like being hot so I have to get out of bed again. Glad it's not too often.

Still most of the time it's cool, me and James are always training now. I find it quite wearing but it feels like James needs it more than me haha.

It's nice with the peace and quiet, lots of people come and fuss me when I'm in the garden and listen to this, James left the kennel at the house. I don't know if he has noticed but I've been sleeping indoors for quite a while now. Knew I would get my way. Ha-ha

It also meant I could redouble my training and with nothing else to concentrate on all of my efforts went into dog training and work.

I used to pick my son up from school a couple of nights a week when allowed and drop him back on my way to work.

It was just me and Hooch now, Hooch became really dependent on me and I probably became the same with him. I couldn't leave him on his own too much so he came everywhere with me and still does to this day.

I missed my kids, after two failed marriages and three children I did a lot of soul searching while I was on my own. I did a lot of a lot of things. When I wasn't working I was with my kids and my life had become very simple.

It was a nice place to live and reasonably peaceful most of the time. I had my own space and was kind of enjoying it except I did swing quite low at times and Hooch was always there. I trained and worked.

Hooch was coming on great and work was good.

I even began to make a few friends on the site, I knew they were really just acquaintances and I didn't plan on sticking around too long. It was freezing in the winter and roasting in the summer.

I recall one summer early evening, a couple of the lads on the site used to pop over and have a beer if I was doing nothing.

Hooch and I had just finished training and the sleeve was on the ground. It was a beautiful evening and the sun was going down after a glorious day. It was just starting to cool down. I had stopped training and cracked open a cold one when a couple of friends walked over.

Chris and Dan sat down in my garden, I said to them both to leave Hooch alone as he had just finished training and was a bit riled up. Hooch was sat with the sleeve between his feet. He had just won it and although breathing hard he was looking extremely intense. His possession increased and since working hard to win the sleeve he didn't look like he was going to give it up to easy.

Then Dan's brother Ben walked over. I issued the same warning, but Ben thought it would be funny to try and grab the sleeve and stare Hooch out. He didn't get close. Hooch was up and barking, sharply and aggressively. I said to Ben "*don't move and don't look him in the eye.*" A look in the eye is as good as a challenge to a dog. Especially when they are in this state of mind.

I wasn't fully concentrating because I was just thinking about his" *hold and bark*" and how this bark, this one right now was cracking. It had the urgency and depth I wanted. I was looking at his body language. Puffed up, mouth open a crack, legs wide apart leaning forward over his prize possession. He was challenging Ben to move, his face wasn't far from Ben's crotch but he was staring up at him and looking him straight in the eye. Daring him to move forward. Almost willing him to.

Then I snapped back and poor old Ben is still stood there trying not to look at Hooch and talking out of the corner of his mouth "*can you stop him*". I called to Hooch and he came over.

Ben was ok just a bit shook up, Hooch went to him for a stroke and Ben bribed him with chips. Lesson no. ?? Always listen.

It was a beautiful moment, not for Ben. But after all the training with Hooch and not being able to get this bark, possession won the day.

As I have said before, if they do what you want them to do just once you can then work on it. As long as you seize the moment or remember it so you can recreate then you can train.

Wow, just had a great training session with James, it's all going well. Suns out, I think I get to have a rest now. Here come the crowd. They always come here. It's like they don't like being at home. Or they've run out of beer.

Only two tonight. Happy days. Stretch out.

Here comes another. This is the one they call Ben. Bless him, just leave me alone. I'm going to have a kip after winning another fight with James.

He's coming for my sleeve. GET OFF, he's only staring me out. What is wrong with these blokes? I'm tired happy and they come along and bugger it up. Gertcha.

So I went back to Mick's with stories of this lovely deep aggressive bark. I recalled it all to Mick. How his bark was so deep, sharp and really sounded aggressive. It was scary to watch let alone be on the wrong side of.

As Hooch barked with his new found skill, he snapped his head forward almost daring the person to move onto it. He had shunted forward when barking at Ben, making Ben give him ground. It was a beautiful scene and I had never seen

Hooch put that sort of aggression into anything. He had played at it and 90% of the time this was all you wanted.

Most people would run, and I had little doubt Hooch would bark up and go in if he had to. But this had been a different side of Hooch. A side that I loved but also a side that needed to be respected.

Also on a plus, Hooch had come away when told and he hadn't actually gone in for the bite. But he was very dominant and very intense.

A couple of things came to me when thinking about it. Ben had gone for the sleeve, so was possession his motivation. Hooch hadn't been possessive of anything before.

Or had it been Ben challenging Hooch and taking his trophy. A combination of the two would be a direct affront to his dominance and status in the pack and Hooch had needed to iron it out.

Not sure, it was going round in my head.

After speaking to Mick, he was happy he knew what it was. So we began.

We started putting different amounts of pressure on Hooch to wind him up, not hurt him or stress him. Hooch had to carry on enjoying what he was doing but balance it with a reality check so Hooch feels a need to bark up and convince the baiter not to come forward.

Mick would wind him up so it was difficult for Hooch to maintain the hold and bark, he wasn't allowed to bite. You can't push them to fail its counterproductive at this stage.

As Hooch's energy was coming up, so was his dominance. His whole demeanour changed. I had never seen Hooch angry. I guess this was it.

The bark, the chest, the pulling forward on the lead. Hooch was daring Mick to move, glaring him in the eye. Hooch was so close to him, every bark was nudging him in the groin, spit was going up his trousers. He would be on the end of the lead but never pulling me, just leaning into it so he could feel my pressure and I could feel his. He had stopped looking at me whilst barking. The feeling of the taught lead was enough to assure him of my presence, he had to know where I was and this was his way of doing it now. It was a growth in confidence and teamwork. It was a lovely thing.

I had never seen Hooch like it, and I have no idea what was going through his head. But he was holding it together, more than that he was enjoying it. This seemed to be his thing. He came up quickly to his aggressive state and would bring it back down just as quick.. Mick would give the signal, Hooch would surge forward with a purpose when I unclipped him. It was like a release for him.

He would hit Mick from only a couple of inches away and powered into him with his back legs. It was like a grudge match, Hooch pushed, powered and then switched and pulled back, finally as Mick had no choice but to come with him, Hooch would power back into him pushing him over.

The first time we got Hooch barking up nicely he hit Mick with a huge amount of power. Mick gave in and the sleeve was relinquished and Hooch walked away with his head held high. I was half expecting him to kick dirt over Mick, the whole struggle had been about 5-10 seconds but it had been completely enthralling for me. This was the new Hooch and this was the Hooch I had built up from the dog that hid behind your legs to the one that would walk away from a scrap like a gladiator with no compunction about doing it again.

With an air of arrogance about him I had fussed him and run around with him and he kept his eyes on Mick, with disdain rather than aggression.

Mick brushed himself down and walked over. Hooch went across to greet him and he got a rub on the head for his troubles. Mick and I were smiling like Cheshire cats.

Oh great, here we go again. Fighting the little fella.

Ok James, hold and bark it is, in I go. Stand off and bark, wait for him to move. I'll have him.

Hang on, what you doing. He's moving, no word from James. He can't do that can he? Still no word. I'll have him. He's staring at me, surely now?? Come on??

Oh my god I'm gonna kill him, he's pushing me back. I can bite him now can't I? Still nothing, I have to give ground. Oh my god, it's an affront. He's still coming. James is backing up, I've never lost James, I can take him. Let me.

This is humiliating, James is letting him win. "Hold"

Thank god, I'll take that ground back.

With Hooch's success with the hold and bark I went back to Micks regularly to reinforce it all.

Hooch was looking into the eyes of the baiter it was important to carry on training with the tug, I had got him to bark and hold really well. He was standing a little bit too far back The plan was to have the tug in front and have him barking. The reward was the bite, but the only way he could have a bite was to look at me in the eye, I would then move my eyebrows and then move the tug.

This meant that as it was repeated he would learn to look at the eyes for the sign to go. This was going great on the tug and with me. So I took him to training. Mick had a couple of friends there so we decided to use them as baiters.

I was stood with Hooch, winding him up, he was getting edgy and bouncing on his front legs as he did. The baiter was moving around and as Hooch lunged forward, I let go.

Hooch went storming towards this guy, but a few foot from him he slowed right down and when in range started mouthing the sleeve, not biting just mouthing. Mick and I looked at each other!! *"What happened I called across"*, Mick looked back at me blankly.

I called Hooch back and tried again. Same thing. I sent him in on the other friend. Same again. No bite just mouthing.
So Mick put the sleeve on and this time Hooch went crashing in on him, as he always did.

Woohoo, loving this training. Loving this winning haha. Mick and James I'm sorted. Sometimes I only have to bark in our games and Mick will back off. Probably because I smashed him that time.

I enjoy training; it's a huge part of my life now. I don't feel like such a goof ball anymore.

I tell you, I used to chew stuff but I have no energy anymore. I feel stimulated and more clever too. James lets me do what I want as long as I do what I'm told when he tells me.

As long as I play the game life is good.

I don't ever seem to lose either. I enjoy most of the stuff we do. I'm not sure about running through tunnels but the rest of it is cool.

Looks like I'm up again, hold on. Who's that??

It's a new bloke, he's not done anything to me. James is telling me to go and bite his arm. The closer I get, I really don't know him. He hasn't done anything to me. Are you sure you want me to bite him. But I don't know him and he's not hurting me, or you for that matter.

No, I'll leave him. I reckon James has made a mistake.

I have often said that I have learnt more from working dogs than most other experiences in my life, I learned that day that when stuff goes left you just have to go with it.

I am a born worrier, analyser. I can't help it; it is just my makeup. I can act like it's not but soon enough I have to take time to worry. This was a worry. Hooch was making amazing progress.

In a few short weeks he had shown me his potential. He had shown me that he had it in him. When I thought that it was in the bag and now it was just tidying up, sharpening him and instilling the suspicion that makes a good working dog, he had thrown me a curve ball. All of the worries of him being nervous, the worries I had on them first few days of backing away from people and keeping his distance all came back to the fore.

Was this nerves? Was this going to rubbish all the training when I find out he would only bite good baiters who knew how to get him going, or people he had bitten before. This is how my mind works, or worked. I catastrophised for days.

I vocalised my worries to Mick, he said it was too early to tell. He could just be having an off day. He can't have off days.

What if his off day ties in with a situation where I need him. Mick was cool about it, he ran over all of the things we had done, all the training we had undergone to cover most eventualities. *"We just need to get him biting different people"*.

I went off with my homework, to get him on as many arms as I could. A few of my friends agreed to be guinea pigs when I explained what had happened.

I phoned Keith. I had worked with Keith a lot, he had baited Max and he had a younger brother called Phillip who Keith assured me would take a few bites. Keith was a no nonsense dog handler. No fancy stuff, just trained his dogs obedience and to bite and let go, he has an awesome dog called Mac.

Mac was a GSD x Malinois if I remember right; he was a great dog with a lovely temperament. He would bite you one minute and cuddle up the next.

Keith and I worked well together as we had many of the same traits and believed very strongly in the same methods for dog handling. It also seemed that the people we met we either both liked or both disliked.

We used to meet up quite regularly if one or the other was working we would pop and see each other for a cuppa so I just used to take Hooch with me.

It was another problem because we would swap over at the business park and end up chatting and me or him would end up leaving an hour late, so we started getting to work half hour early so we could spread our chat over both of our shifts. I still class him as a friend and he has helped me many times with the dogs and just with general advice.

After discovering Hooch's new hang up, I was frustrated to say the least. I never took it out on Hooch; it was just a hurdle to be got over. Not an easy one because I had never had this problem.

Most dogs when trained to bite rarely become fussy about who to bite. But Hooch was a sensitive little soul so I took advice and decided to go ahead with Plan: bite anyone who's willing.

I met Keith at Chievely services near Newbury. Keith and I used to go training near there and so we met first. Keith had Phillip with him and found a grassy area to practice on.

Keith decided to offer the dubious honour of taking bites to Phillip. Phillip was quite new to baiting at the time; he could wind dogs up and knew the signals.

Phillip started moving around and once again Hooch started bouncing and getting geared up. He bounced on his front feet making his guttural noise from deep in his throat. It was a lovely noise and my confidence started returning, maybe it was an off day. Hooch was doing what he did normally. I was chuffed and confused in the very same thoughts. He dropped his head, straightening his neck to exude his loud bark. He was looking just the same as he always did in these situations. Phillip hadn't put any pressure on and was a distance away so Hooch didn't feel threatened. I waited for his raised arm and let Hooch go in the vain hope that he would hit Phillip hard. He went tearing off and lunged straight at Phillip. Hooch grabbed his arm and kept pumping to run through him. It was a great bite, straight to the back of his mouth and when he didn't knock Phillip over he started ragging him around.

Most dogs have the ability to use their balance and force to wrong foot you, they pull as hard as they can and when you pull back they go with you or the opposite. It's clever and it works, this is what Hooch was doing.

In the meantime I was smiling like a Cheshire cat, I hadn't seen Hooch with this much energy and aggression. He was doing great, Keith tapped me on the shoulder telling me to get Hooch of his brother.

I snapped back to reality and called Hooch, he came straight over puffing and panting but you could tell he was happy with his workout. His tail was wagging and his chest was puffed out.

I was so happy, but don't count your chickens. You have to be as confident in your dog as possible when you are counting on them as much as we do as Dog Handlers.

Ah, it seems I may have been mistaken in my assessment of my remit. It would seem that James can send me in on whoever.

138

We had a long drive today and there was these two Welsh blokes. One put that tug thing on his arm and started waving it about. This is always a pre cursor to me playing with their arms.

It seems like ages since I played that game, well it's been since I didn't want to bite that nice bloke. Hmmm

Anyway, I thought I would have a go. It was great fun, I didn't knock him over. He was strong for a wiry bloke but I did pull him about a bit. I loved it, and to add to it. James looked chuffed to bits with me.

Maybe I'm just supposed to bite whoever he tells me. I'll try that from now on. He was so happy bless him.

The next day after working all night I drove up to Birmingham to see my friend Phil, this would be a great test for Hooch.

Dogs know people, I've mentioned that. Hooch was a strong dog, and putting his wobble aside he had always attacked on command with no hesitation. But I couldn't forget his nerves when I first got him and his wobble the previous week. This workout was to get him over it.

Phillip had baited Hooch well and for Hooch it was a game, Hooch had really worked Phillip, I knew it wouldn't be like this with Phil. Phil was a big guy, and he was a solid baiter.

Just like in life with people. Management is a matter of knowing and understanding the person you are managing, whether you are managing up or down this is true.

I knew Keith and Phillip would play with Hooch and bait him well and bait him gently. It was one way to get the best out of him and give him a positive association to the bite.

Phil was very different, Phil has a very confident and strong persona, and this would be picked up straight away by Hooch and would possibly put him backwards.

I had discussed with Phil that the minute Hooch backed up or showed any signs of backing up Phil was to act beaten, turning sideways and making yourself smaller will make the dog believe they are winning and hence give them the confidence to finish the job.

That is of course if Hooch even latched on. I wasn't too worried about him biting Phillip, but Phil was a different kettle of fish.

This was a big test. Like I say, I needed Hooch to bite on command no matter what so I needed to test him on different levels of threat and more importantly different people. But I also needed to be careful not to overdo it and put him off biting or even worse make him overly aggressive.

This is a balancing act, very much like people you get the best out of your dog by knowing how to manage him/her and where his weakness and strengths are. This would just go along with all the other balancing acts and plate spinning you do as a Dog handler, training your own dog is hard.

It involves knowing the boundaries and where to stop and where to carry on and all of this is based on what you want out of your dog and what your dog's capabilities are.

I have seen many good dogs ruined by bad or impatient training, and many incapable dogs paraded in front of people as if they are something special.

I wanted Hooch to be something special but I also didn't want to make the mistake of assuming he could do all the things I wanted him to. I needed to know and I wanted him to protect me, not because he was trained to but because he saw the leadership in me and it becomes second nature to him.

So we drove from Bracknell to Smethwick. Apart from Phil I had a couple of acquaintances up there so I was hoping I could set Hooch on a few people.

We got to Phil's and had our catch up. After a little while we decided we could get going with Hooch. He seemed comfortable running about with Phil's dogs so we put them away and Phil got the sleeve ready.

I don't see this as dissimilar to people. If after a setback you take your staff or your children and try forcing them back into doing the task you were asking them to do and the task they failed at last time. You will just pile the pressure on and set them up to fail.

Step back. Look at the situation and see if there is something you can do to ease them back into it. You don't have to discuss it with them. If you see a way of getting them to do the same task or a similar one that will build that confidence up. Allow them to attach a positive to it and reinforce that positive. Take it back to basics if you have to. You may have missed a step or assumed understanding of a step.

I was holding on to Hooch, he was glaring at Phil. He seemed ready for this, as soon as I clipped him up he seemed to take on a different persona.

He looked at Phil with menace in his eyes; he straight away came to attention and seemed to be ready. Phil's bulk and posture didn't seem to concern him. Hooch was leaning forward and pushing out his chest.

Hooch always became tall and rigid when he knew he was up for a bite. Here it was that lovely upright confident stand. Phil was starting to move now from side to side. Hooch's interest was peaking and that low growl was starting to settle in the bottom of his throat.

Phil made the signal and I let Hooch go. He cleared the few feet between Phil and I in staggering speed. He hit Phil and Phil doubled immediately doubled over.

The bite was great and as he went in he turned the sleeve over and hit Phil in the sternum with his head. It was a great action, complete accident but awesome and Phil dropped to one knee.

He let Hooch win the sleeve not sure he had a choice and Hooch came away with the sleeve and his tail wagging came straight back to me.

Phil was still on one knee stringing a long line of expletives together because Hooch had winded him good and proper. I was hoping he would get up ok. I think Hooch was thinking the same because he was up for another.

Haha, this is great. I understand now. I am just to bite anyone James tells me to. I know this because when I did it to that big bloke.

James let out a laugh that sounded like it was more of relief and happiness than a joke.

I thought I'd throw in a ninja head butt too. Big fella is still on the floor which is a shame because I thought I would get a good fight out of him. I love wrestling them and winning that tug thing. It's the most fun.

So I think it's all cleared up now, he says "hold him" I bite them. Doesn't matter who, or if they are my friend or not. I just do it.

If he had just said this earlier. Oh well. Got it now.

There was absolutely no hesitation or caution with this bite. I was very happy. I needed him to go out and do more but this was a great start. Operation Bite anyone was going well.

Later on that day we were going to a site Phil was working and going to put Hooch on another couple of guys. All being well it would be a successful weekend.

Phil and I went over to the site Phil was working at, at the site were a couple of guys we had worked with in the past and one decided he would take a bite.

I won't lie, I was beginning to really enjoy this. Hooch had a power and intensity that comes from the fact that his bite training had started so late that he bit instinctively. Nobody had messed him up, not had too much pressure put on him at an early age. He did what dogs do. He did it well.

I would like to be able to explain this feeling but I can't. When your dog goes in to the bite and really commits himself bursting with confidence. You do look inward and have a smile to yourself. I don't know if it's a macho thing, pride of him doing what you've trained him or a bit of both. I'm not sure. But whatever it is it's an amazing feeling.

We went to a site in Birmingham somewhere; it was a derelict office building and a car park.

We had a chat with the guys and then set up for the bite. Phil was telling them about his experience with Hooch and one of the guys said "*that's alright, I'll show him*" Alarm bells rang. Macho Dog Handlers who are willing to push your dog back because they have something to prove are the last thing you need.

The essence of this is, if the dog is a threat to them. Some people think it will be cool to act tough and force your dog backwards by getting in their face. They turn the pressure up. It's not helpful and unless your dog is bombproof. It just shouldn't be done. Especially with Hooch just getting the hang of it, he didn't need to chalk up any losses. Like I say it's all about confidence. It's very easy to knock a new dog's confidence with a negative session.

I spoke to him and said he was quite new to all this and to take it steady. Hooch must win because of what had happened over the last week.

He got himself ready and I got Hooch out. Hooch was his usual self upon sight of the baiter and sleeve in front of him.

His tail started going and you could see from his posture his excitement levels were raising.

The baiter waved his arm and Hooch by this point was grumbling and bouncing. At the right moment I let him go issuing the command, "*hold him.*"

Hooch stormed in, took the sleeve lovely. The baiter started wrestling him, Hooch had gone in well, but over a short distance he hadn't got the momentum up to hit him really hard. But Hooch was hanging on and the baiter was tugging and pulling.

Hooch wouldn't let go while the baiter was moving because like all dogs, he's not letting go until he has won. So the wrestling went on. "*stand still, I'll out him*" I shouted. The baiter had other ideas and started pushing Hooch with his knees.

Pushing dogs around while baiting them is a popular technique because it doesn't hurt them but it does start putting a little bit of pressure on them. "*stand still*" I called again.

We were at a stalemate because Hooch won't let go while there is still movement and the baiter wasn't letting up. Then Hooch almost ran at him off balancing him and the baiter had to let go or fall. The baiter let go.

I called Hooch back and put him in the van telling him what a good boy he had been. He had won, and he hadn't at any point lost his nerve. This was a great win, though I didn't want it to happen like that. It had and there was nothing I could do about it now but tell Hooch what a good lad he had been.

I went back and had a chat with the baiter about controlling his ego. There really is no need for this type of training. The quickest way to train a dog is slowly. Give it time, have some patience and do it the right way. If you rush head long into training you can put a dog off for life or if you train badly it can take twice as long to undo what you have done.

People are the same, make training interactive and fun. Not stupid fun, but it is a fact that information learnt when having fun is so much more likely to be retained. Too much pressure and people and dogs just dread the next course.

I used to go to dog training at different places all the time and many of the trainers and presenters in the world could learn a lot from dog trainers. High tempo, fun, no monotones because dogs won't respond. All the things you do to effectively train your dog works in a similar way with people.

I will never forget I did a course a few years ago, the guy taking the course just read from his notes for the whole day. It was awful. I don't remember anything from that course. Not a jot. I remember the room and I kind of remember what the course was about, roughly. I even remember lunch. But the content I have no clue.

In contrast I did a sales skills course. It was also awful, the content was rubbish and not my cup of tea. It was all about seeing customers and before you went to see them you would put your cape on because you are a super hero.

It didn't work, it taught me nothing. I won't take any of those practices on, however. I remember all of it. The gent that took the course was full of relentless enthusiasm and it was interactive, we were indoors outdoors, throwing thought balls to each other.

The point is it was up tempo and whether I agree with the content or not I listened and understood.

When I help people with their dogs, it is so hard to get people. Especially men to put the enthusiasm in, the overstated movement. For fear of embarrassing themselves.

But if you were a dog would you listen to your owner's monotone voice nagging at you to do the same thing over and over. Or would you like quick movements, commands with urgency and tempo and high pitched praise. I know it doesn't all work in a training room with people but it's not far different.

I don't know what's going on here. It's like a bite fest. One minute I'm doing none and then all the time.

I think it is because I was always supposed to just bite. That must be it. I've got it. But only when I'm told or people are being idiots.

Like that last bloke. I had to fight him. He wasn't having any of it. It was a good fight though, good fun. I had to do a little Hooch ninja but doesn't matter. I won again and that's all that matters.

I wonder if there is anyone who can beat me. The last bloke came close, I was wondering when he would stop fighting. When he fell over I guess ha-ha

Phil and I left the site laughing to each other. We both had an idea that he would put the pressure on but both of us thought that with a conversation and getting our point across we could rule this out. Turns out some people will always work with their own agenda.

We both found it funny and were just chuffed that Hooch had dealt with it and dealt with it well.

It was a strange week, It had started out with Hooch worrying me for his not biting and ended up with him taking more pressure than I expected he could and coming out on top.

It just shows that worrying will get you nowhere. Dogs will do what dogs will do and the only thing you can influence is the foundations that you should have helped build with the training to make them robust.

There are many similarities in people here of course.

The foundations you build for your children are similar to dogs as I said earlier. It is all about giving them as much exposure to different experiences and just like dogs, there is social training, so loads of time with other kids and adults so they learn how to socialise appropriately and so social occasions are not daunting.

Environmental such as fireworks, noisy occasions, letting them meet animals, people, and swimming. The list is endless and again like dogs you cannot expose them to every situation they could ever land in. But you can get them used to

144

many and this way they will be robust and would deal with new experiences with little or no heed.

This leads me on well to my next story. It's just like I planned it.

Phil and I were working that night in Answorth Park. I remember following Phil to the venue and we pulled up at some lights. I looked around and instinctively pushed the central locking button. I hadn't been to this event before but if the roads leading to it were anything to go by. It was going to be fun.

We both pulled up at Answorth Park, Phil had worked here before and knew it well so he took the lead and I just followed him about. I was only an extra dog for later on if it all went wrong.

I was still on a bit of a high after Hooch's earlier success. I wandered around the park with Phil and orientated myself. It was a nice big park, loads of land to run the dogs later when it was all locked up. Took Hooch for a few walks and he seemed interested and lively.

It was all going well. The gates got locked and Phil said it was time to let the dogs have a runabout.

I let Hooch out and he jumped out of the car and instantly looked apprehensive.

This was a thing I had come to expect from Hooch and was hoping that his environmental training would really come into effect with this problem. Hooch always spent a bit of time getting used to an area and was never at ease until he had investigated a new area fully.

This is all due to a lack of training in his formative years. Again this is something you can turn around over time but it's much quicker and less problematic if you do this early as I've explained.

The same obviously goes for kids. I don't know if this is because of our thought process's as we get older. Maybe dogs start to weigh up risk and reward as we humans do but it does seem as they get older they are more hesitant to new experiences. But if you do your environmental training right you they never lose this confidence.

After a few walks around Hooch had the hang of it and was fine.

Hooch and I had a peaceful evening followed by a long journey back home.

This was the journey home that I remember vividly being the time I spent thinking about the contents of this book. I have one of them annoying memories that remembers everything you don't need nor probably want to remember and exactly the circumstances but very little else.

I remember driving back from Birmingham and I was speaking to my Dad on the earpiece thing that were all the rage, with my coffee and red bulls on the go. I remember the car I was driving and even the conditions but I couldn't tell you what year it was or what I was doing outside of that moment.

Anyway, I had my conversation and was driving and suddenly, like an epiphany it came to me that all of this training was very adaptable to humans.

I will say that though I don't remember which year it was, I do remember it was a while. Probably 6 or 7 years ago maybe a bit more. It's taken me this long to bring it to fruition. But as I have always been told, things happen when they are supposed to, mainly when you are ready. This in hindsight is not backed up by my experience. But let's keep this book smiley.

Going back to the point. I had been explaining my situation with Hooch to my Dad, who as I have mentioned before was probably bored rigid because I talk about dogs a lot and Dad doesn't share my passion. But what my Dad does do very well is convert it to people, because he understands people as he used to manage them.

So this is kind of where the idea germinated. The seed was planted and many other clichés. But what it did was it brought the two elements together.

I believe we were talking about Hooch and his apprehension of new sites, and how well he had done on the bite work. I was very proud of his bite work and as such wanted it run out that I had overcome his problem.

A little bit like Hooch winning his sleeve and running around with the sleeve in his mouth, I wanted to puff my chest out and show off my trophy a bit.

I had spoken about his training and how it was an odd way of doing it but it's not a one size fits all so you have to be flexible and a bit reactive to the dog's needs. Dad instantly turned it and understood that when training people it was the same. You train lots of people it's one size fits all. Just on a practical level. Like a puppy training course. Lots of puppies.

Here is the most effective way of training them, it has the best results across the board. One to one training you can be reactive, a bit different and solve individual challenges with slightly less used or known methods.

I'm training a couple at the moment. They have a lovely little Dachshund, He's a nice little dog and he is clever. He is a little aggressive to other dogs in certain circumstances; the circumstances seem to change regularly. Or regularly enough to never find a common cause.

So like fixing a car engine or as I have spoken to in this book. We are taking it back to basics. We are concentrating on sit, heel, down. Putting the dog in positions with commands.

This will do a couple of things. Firstly it will bring a well behaved dog, you can get the dog to be where you want the dog at any time. This makes owning a dog simpler. Life goes on if they don't have this training but with the training it greases the wheels.

But mainly, it teaches your dog who is in charge. You are the one putting them into positions. You are dictating when and where. With the right training you are also doing it in a fun way, a respectful way.

So like a good boss, they tell you to do something and you know you have to do it but it is like you have been requested, not ordered. When you do it you will get the praise you deserve and the warm feeling for doing a good job well.

Thirdly and never to be forgotten, you are giving the dog confidence in his ability to do things right. He constantly gets it right. The reason he constantly gets it right is because he is ignored when he does it wrong.

Any attention is good attention, people used to say that about kids. Dogs are no different. But no attention, well that's just rubbish. So give them attention and tell them they did it right. If in training they get it wrong, just keep walking. The best you will do by lambasting them is add pressure and dissolve confidence. The worst you will do is train them to do it wrong in which case you have a good few sessions of retraining.

Like I say he is lovely, the couple listen very well and understand fully that this is more about them learning to handle the dog than it is Marley learning. It is all going great but as with people we have had to modify training.

You can't modify training in group sessions effectively and just like people dogs learn at different paces but when you are teaching people to teach dogs, well now you have dogs learning at different paces, and people teaching them and learning themselves at different paces.

He is learning very simple commands and also commands he probably knows only too well but chooses not to do all of the time. The idea of the training is to empower the owners by taking on challenges that are easy wins.

147

Let's get the dog doing what you ask; it doesn't actually matter about the complexity of the task. It only matters that Marley does as he is told when he is told and that he does it willingly with no conflict or pushing about.

When you start pushing and ordering, you achieve nothing. The dog/person does as he is told because he has no choice. It is very similar to not trusting confessions from people subjected to torture. They have to say something so they do, it can't be relied upon because they were under duress.

It is similar with training. If you have a dog and you tell it to sit. The dog knows what sit means but acts as if it doesn't. You push its bum to the floor.

Now the question is, have you made your dog sit? Yes, if you put aside the physical consequences of putting pressure on their bones. You have made your dog sit. He/she will get up just as quick and next time you do it you will have to push him again because he has learnt nothing because you have just forced him into a position.

You know when you are seeking understanding from someone and you ask them to summarise what you just said. Getting a dog to sit is similar. Without the end result being him sitting of his own volition and understanding consequence you can be sure of absolutely nothing.

If you look at a contrary way of doing it. When you have the dog near you, you put a treat right by their nose, just above it, you move it back with your hand as you move your hand the dog is moving with you, it doesn't want to miss this. As you go up and back the dogs bum naturally goes down. It's simple, the reward, the dog has a positive association to the word sit. A few more times and he/she will be doing it no problem.

It's no different with staff or children. Always take time to get to know your staff, you should already have this in the bag with your kids. With staff if you are training a small group you need to know them so you can train them most effectively.

At the company I work for, we have large events and they come on to smoke and music and disco lights. You can literally see the mood change and not for the better. It may work in America but we don't work like it over here. We are much more miserable and seem happier with the bad news section than the back slapping get out of your seats and roar like lions bit.

Assess your team, work out how to motivate them because one size really doesn't fit all and at best its dull for the people it doesn't fit and at worst the content never gets delivered and actually becomes an irritant to them because of the style of delivery and becomes completely counterproductive.

148

How many people reading this have children that they describe as chalk and cheese?

I would hazard a guess that it applies to nearly everyone with more than two. And how many times are you surprised that the same method of motivation doesn't work for both, the same method of discipline doesn't work for both.

I get for practicalities and for a uniform front that consequences for similar actions must remain the same for two siblings and in fact co-workers too. But the negative association doesn't have to.

I have two daughters and both are delightful in their own ways. They are also a nightmare in their own ways.

That is the key phrase, in their own ways. I have one daughter that tries to convince everyone she is an angel. She is not stalwart and believes the point of having a mind is so she can change it if she feels the need. She listens to most opinions and puts together a good argument back. If it is something she believes in.

Now until a few years ago you could sit her down, talk to her about the consequences of her actions, and walk away from her knowing she would think on it. She wouldn't always avoid those consequences but she would give them thought at least.

My other daughter there was never any notice if she was going to misbehave. Sometimes you were lucky if you found out that day. She was stubborn, challenging and stalwart. She gave most people a run for their money because she wouldn't give up without a fight. It got her in a lot of trouble. However if she had voiced her questioning nature appropriately it would have been an attribute.

You see the difference and everyone has a gift and a skill, it may not be what you want it to be, but you have to roll with it. But also people have a specific way of learning. This is not news to anyone who has presented or read anything about training with visual, audio and kinaesthetic.

But there is so much more to it than that. There is mood, listening styles.

I remember watching an amazing man give a speech at an event of ours. He had an amazing story, all true about his expeditions. He was a famous man for his achievements. It is something I find amazing, man against the elements, mental and physical challenges and would be something I would always remember. I cannot even remember where he walked!!

I watched Nicholas McCarthy, a one handed pianist do a presentation about overcoming adversity. I remember his story, I even remember his jokes. He played piano at the end and I don't do classical music. But the passion, the tempo, the story behind it all. I was taken with it and though the subject is of little or no interest I remember it vividly.

Nothing to do with styles because I am Kinaesthetic allegedly.

It's all about being honest and passionate about what you are talking about. Confidence matters don't get me wrong but I would rather listen to a man who was humble about his own achievements than someone else that has found a three minute clip of a race and describe the emotions going through each man's head whilst running a race they have never competed in talking about people they have never met.

You see similar to dogs, we have instincts. They lead us to make reasonably quick decisions and judgements.

If you don't like someone. If they are too polished, there is a lot they have to achieve to bring your defences down. Because as a rule us humans have always rallied behind the underdog. We like all that and if someone is too polished, in our minds it almost comes across as conceited or arrogant.

We as a race also know who we want to lead, it is too ingrained in us to let go. But unfortunately material things and other agendas change our minds from who we would look too naturally.

It all gets complicated and it is a skill of the trainer to keep up and down with everyone and adapt his/her teaching technique to all of the people he is teaching to. It's very difficult but also comes very naturally to some.

So this is the benefit of one to one training and this is what I was chatting about to my Dad when it came to me that dogs and people are not to dissimilar. In fact if you noticed in the last couple of paragraphs I switched between people and dogs several times and it makes no difference.

I speak about these with experience from both sides of the top table. I can genuinely say it is a rare skill to find a presenter who gets the audience right every time. I could refer you to example after example of what seemed like a great subject presented poorly and a subject that I wouldn't give you tuppence for but made interesting by a great presentation.

I am not unfairly criticising. I am not a good presenter myself. That's why I avoid it on all subjects. But I can train, in a field with dogs and their owners because this is where I am comfortable, passionate and honest.

But let me let you into a secret. Preparation is important. But so is the ability to wing it. You have to fake confidence until you build it up by positive associations. It's not unnatural. It is difficult for everyone.

But one more little hint.

The unnecessary use of maxims. I hope this isn't just my pet hate.

An inspirational famous saying. Yes, "keep your powder dry", "march separately, fight together", "to take the island, burn the boats." Stop.

Not much of this is transferable to the world of Tupperware sellers, or FMCG companies. The only sin I find worse than this is the use of a maxim only to be followed by an explanation.

You've now implied I am at battle with another Tupperware seller or a rep from another company and then insulted me a second time by thinking I didn't understand the meaning of your moving maxim. Neither of which are probably true.

So in short, as a presenter or trainer. You first have to sell yourself to the audience, customer or dog. Without them liking, respecting or listening to you. You have no chance at all.

Once you have won them, then you need to listen to them. What makes them tick? What are they listening for? What is the hook? Where is the value?

Once you have worked out the hook, you know what makes them tick. How do you bring that to life in the remit of your training/presenting?

Now put it in a format that works for them, high tempo, slow it down, interactive.

All of this works for everybody we are talking about. Customers, colleagues, managers, dogs, dog owners. They all must see a value in what you are doing. You must reinforce that value so they know what to expect.

But most of all. If you cannot fulfil that value, commitment. Tell them, tell them why, and be honest because you must assume they have come to you for that honesty because this isn't something they can fix themselves or they would have done.

A relationship in the animal world as in the people world can take a lifetime to build and a moment to shatter. So stay honest. Honest about their expectations and yours which should align if you have listened or watched well enough.

To be dishonest or disingenuous to either human or dog will be found out and makes for a very short term relationship in any situation you enter into.

One thing I have learned is that people and dogs have an amazing ability to learn, and in the main most want to. So when you train or teach somebody something it is always a good idea to summarize to see if it is understood. It is

151

easy, especially with a mind like mine that you can miss a step whilst digressing about something else.

In many cases this is the reason people miss things and understanding is lacking.

I was talking about housetraining puppies to a couple of dog handlers once. One of the gents there said *"the very best way to train a dog to toilet outside is"* we all looked at him in anticipation, mainly because there are so many methods. But here is another one. Just what the world needs *" if you come home and your dog has messed on the floor, get a newspaper, roll it up nice and tight"* oh dear lord. Here we go, lets punish him/her for something he can't even remember doing *"and hit yourself as hard over the head as you can because you've done something wrong in his training"*

Oh, right. He was right. It applies just as well for training with people. If your training isn't working, important things are getting missed. Look inward. What have you missed? What haven't you told them or have you not conveyed it in a way that makes sense or encourages them to learn.

If there is a setback, just step back. Take another look.

These are the beginnings of Hooch and I and the friendship we built. This friendship has continued to build over the years, and will continue.

But I think now is a natural moment in the book to take a break and summarise what we have learnt.

Although this really is just skimming the surface of what I mean about our similarities and the way we can use each other to learn.

I have embraced this in my teaching of Hooch and my relationship with him.

You should have noticed in my book, the subject is set around our relationship with dogs. I speak about teaching children and understanding them. Part of understanding them would be to show us how to motivate them and empower them to do the things they want to and the courage not to shy away from their convictions.

Training dogs with the respect and getting the best out of them, training them slowly and not expecting them to deal with situations you haven't prepared them for. Training them with respect and dignity also builds your bond and brings you a closeness that I can testify to where Hooch as close as dammit reads my mind.

Your staff and colleagues need this respect and to be treated in a way that is conducive to your working relationship but also most efficient for your company or department.

These things won't always work and there will always be setbacks, but this is what utopia looks like in a business setting.

The greatest thing about putting it into a dog analogy is, you've listened because I haven't mentioned a psychologist, a motivational speaker, a text book to read. Because innately we all have this in our brains. It is instinctive and we can do it.

This is not a revolution and I am not trying to turn you all into "cynics" but I think if you went half way, if you looked at your dog or your pet and realised that you could take some learning from his way and the way you treat him. You could make life a smoother ride and take some of the stress out of parenthood, work, and management.

We must get into a more humble mind-set. You see my belief is that every animal and every person has something to teach us. We only watch dogs because they are socialised. But all animals have something we can learn from. Even if that something is something that is not achievable by us it is incredible to absorb that knowledge and maybe achieve a small amount of humility when we realise that as a race we are probably not as perfectly suited to our environment as other animals are to theirs and we are most definitely not as civilised as many animals. We may be more advanced but if you class measure civilisation by morality then many animals if not all are winning that race.

Take your dog to a training class, listen to the instructor. Work out where the dog training overlaps working with your kids to get something done. Or even how you could use some methods in their basic form to help with relationships in the office.

Diogenes was a Greek philosopher, read up about him. He is talking about the same virtues as this book although I am not going to sleep in a vase and eat with my hands any time soon.

He is very interesting and made it his life's mission to live a simpler life like the dog.

Many anecdotes of Diogenes refer to his dog-like behaviour, and his praise of a dog's virtues. It is not known whether Diogenes was insulted with the epithet "doggish" and made a virtue of it, or whether he first took up the dog theme himself. When asked why he was called dog he replied, "I fawn on those who give me anything, I yelp at those who refuse, and I set my teeth in rascals."[17] Diogenes believed human beings live artificially and hypocritically and would do well to study the dog. Besides performing natural body functions in public with ease, a dog will eat anything, and make no fuss about where to sleep. Dogs live in the present without anxiety, and have no use for the pretensions of abstract philosophy. In addition to these virtues, dogs are thought to know instinctively who is friend and who is foe.[51] Unlike human beings who either dupe others or are duped, dogs will give an honest bark at the truth. Diogenes stated that "other dogs bite their enemies, I bite my friends to save them."[52]

The term "Cynic" itself derives from the Greek word κυνικός, kynikos, "dog-like" and that from κύων, kyôn, "dog" (genitive: kynos)

It is a wonderful thought and probably similar to communism will never work. Practicality dictates that we cannot fulfil this state of "dog-like" living.

This isn't a cult and I am only conveying to you a way of looking at life and a way of carrying yourself that is calmer and more effective. It really is as simple as that.

This is the beauty of it. Simplicity and common sense.

To live in a jar and urinate in the street is not necessary but the idea of using our K9 friend's outlook on life can help us in many parts of our lives.

The fact that merely having a dog in your life enables you to live a less stressful and longer life.

Learn a lesson from your dog, "whatever life throws at you, kick grass over that s*** and move on"

Everything has Changed

I will quietly listen to you and pass no judgement,
nor will your spoken words be repeated.
I will remain ever silent, ever vigilant, ever loyal.
When our time together is done and you move on in the world.
Remember me with kind thoughts and tales.
For a time we were unbeatable, nothing passed among us undetected.

I believe we are at that stage due to the training and the time spent where Hooch is almost telepathic. It is quite incredible the bond you can have with an animal that cannot understand any of the spoken language you use. Which brings one point very much to the forefront of my mind. If we can have such great relationships with dogs and they don't actually understand our spoken language. Is it because of this or despite this?

I believe Hooch probably understands me and my moods better than most people but I can only guess this is because he pays no heed to what I am saying and instead understands what I really mean.

In short Hooch and I were a cracking team then and are a cracking team now. Hooch had the moves and relished training. I enjoyed having him around and was enjoying having a dog that I had trained and between his natural temperament and the tidying up of his natural skills he had become quite a Protection dog. Always alert, always up for training and mainly well behaved.

We had an understanding probably born of routine where he seemed to know what I was going to do before I did. It gives you a great comfort when a lot of the time you don't even have to say anything, he just gets it. I think it was a symptom of the fact we spent very little time apart.

In life and with staff, children and customers we are constantly expected to make other people understand. I for one can waffle for a long time trying to make people really understand what I mean. Hooch just gets it. I don't have to explain it and it wouldn't do any good if I did. So I think this takes the pressure of my relationship. I can dismiss his foolishness with *"what do you expect, he's a dog"* I can't do that with my kids.

In the couple of years Hooch had aged mentally and nicely. He had a strong wise head on his shoulders and seemed to be able to sum up situations very quickly. He was confident and didn't rise up quickly when encountering people.

He would be watchful and standoff but if I said "*be nice*" it meant he could go and see them. He loved nothing more than a fuss which was lucky because wherever we went he got a lot of fuss.

He seemed to give off an aura when he was calm. An aura that seemed to work even for people a little bit scared of dog. I think it's his face.

His instinct and behaviour in situations was calm and steady and took from me the cues to become aggressive which was exactly what I wanted. You have to know your dog isn't a loose cannon when you are working amongst crowds of people.

I had every faith in him and it seemed like he had every faith in me.

After a few years of working I had got to know many many people in Dog handling and worked for most of them. I always prided myself on my reliability and the standard of training and therefore the standard of my work. Now I had the dog to back it all up I was happy. I had done a few events and had been the first into trouble with no hesitation of what Hooch could do and also how he looked to the people the other end of the lead.

He hadn't bitten and nor had he needed to. He was a big lad, he was now well exercised and fit. He was obedient and sharp and always looked good as I used to groom him nightly. It was part of our routine because Hooch loves a brush.

We have continued to work without break and everything has just trickled along. Unfortunately the Russians work came to an end. It was good while it lasted but as always there is little you can do when you are self-employed.

I was replaced by a firm that were bidding for half what I was getting paid and offering about the same. The draw was too much for my boss. I get it, and why not. He was rich for these reasons.

The entire site had changed as he had bought next door and next door to that so he could build a guest house and a helipad.

The new firm had offered him two dog handlers for what he was paying me. I told him it was a false economy but not wanting to bad mouth an outfit and knowing he would also get a sizeable discount on his insurance for two dog handlers. I decided my time was probably up with him anyway.

I recall him asking me once while we were sat in his garden looking out over his lake with a cup of tea. "*What do I pay you for*" It was a fair enough question. And though I did a lot above and beyond my own job, like watering his plants when the gardener wanted time off. What did he pay me for, walking around his grounds? Being a deterrent? I used to give his kids lifts to school and would make sure everything was good when the gardener or estates manager were off.

In the end I diplomatically answered *"you pay me for what I am capable off should the need arise."*

Sounded sinister enough and tough enough. I was happy with my reply. Of course it was true too. We were paid to attend site and sit there in case something happened.

I enjoyed the time I worked for him and it was exceptional to have on your C.V. not to mention a beautiful site with very little expectation except to look after his family and property. He was fair and firm and most of all he paid on time.

I was lucky enough to have kept a good job going for two years. That was good, watching friends and colleagues working short term jobs made me uneasy and though I enjoyed the variety living on your own came with certain responsibilities which would have made erratic work difficult to stomach.

Hooch's training took off and with the challenges and obstacles we overcame, it is still just myself and him.

Hooch's temperament has stayed very much the same, he has turned into Mr dependable has rarely left my side. He really has taken to life with just me and him. We have our little routines, he is always by the bed when I wake up and he pushes his head into mine for a good morning nose rub or something. I have no idea where that came from but it certainly seems like it isn't going away anytime soon after nine odd years of doing it I would think there was something wrong if he didn't.

He sits out in the garden with me and relaxes a lot. He has now got a waiting list, people are literally waiting for me to not be able to look after him or something so they can take him on. It's a bit crazy. Such is Hooch's draw to people. I think it is because he looks like Scooby Do.

I have worked several different jobs, the beauty of having put myself out there in the dog world and having a great reputation and having burnt no bridges.

I was lucky enough to work at a beautiful prestigious college in Wokingham Berkshire.I had just started working with Hooch to get him to scent and track. The amount of different environments and smells would make it really hard for Hooch which meant as he progressed I could put him near the kitchen or the rifle range all of which had scents that would be off putting for him. The whole idea like all training is that as they get good at it you up the stakes to progress them.

At the beginning I spent my whole nights just wandering around with Hooch to get a good idea of the site, there was always something going on to get Hooch around people and crowds. You couldn't tire Hooch, he had an amazing amount of energy for a large breed and took to training like a game. His energy would go sky high and the trick was actually to bring his energy down so his obedience would be accurate and controlled. Then instantaneously you could bring his energy up for tug work.

I asked colleagues like Keith to pop into work at different times if they were at a loose end and jump out on us while we were working.

They had to keep at a safe distance because Hooch would view this as a real threat and I couldn't guarantee their safety if they were too close.

The idea of surprising us was to get and keep Hooch's suspicion up, all too often on a regular site your dog could switch off due to the familiarity of the site and goings on.

The other aim and just as important was to really nail down Hooch's and my reaction to this so it was second nature.

A lot goes through your head when you come across a situation, and like I covered earlier in the book there are dog handlers and Dog Handlers, a dog handler takes his dog to the very basic of what is necessary. Many would just have a mean streak from being pressured too much and just bark up, possibly bite. But I have always believed myself to be a professional, I spent a long time training my dog and making sure his temperament right so he reacts as he should in these situations.

You see, you do not want teeth on a lead. When you are working a site with other people possibly wandering around you need a sociable dog. One that will assess a situation.

If someone jumps out on you, it could be one of the college kids or staff. They could be up to no good but your dog is there to defend itself and you and this is the only situation you can send them in. If a couple of kids are off having a smooch, or smoking this doesn't warrant holes in their arms. So the idea is Hooch would pick up on people and be suspicious. Indicate to me that they were there and keep his eye on them. I was then to challenge what was going on and make the decision accordingly.

Most Dog Handlers I know will tell you 90% of our job is just wandering round and keeping the peace by way of a deterrent. 9% of the job if it's that much would be barking up in a situation keeping people in an area until help arrived and you could get them detained safely. 1% you would actually look to bite, and no Dog Handlers actually want their dogs to bite but it is essential they have the ability to do it and do it properly.

Obviously when you hide someone up and they jump out on you they make a load of noise and wave about to wind your dog up. It is all a game, but it happens

159

so quickly and it has to, because everything you do in those milliseconds is hugely important. You have to react quickly, practically Hooch was about 52kg with four wheel drive and a low centre of gravity with reactions that most people are envious of. If you don't react straight away and plant your feet, he is taking you with him and you no longer have any control.

So it is important to know your surroundings, to know you are not too close to either side of the path or road so you have the time and distance to react.

To do this training you can really see what control you have of your dog in that split second you need it. The last thing you want is an illegal bite, the damage these dogs can do is scary and especially if it was a child, like I say Hooch is 8st odd and more powerful and in many cases larger than most kids. It doesn't bear thinking about.

As a Dog Handler it is a great asset to be able to do the physical side of the role as second nature. If you naturally look for open windows, lights where lights shouldn't be or no lights where there should be. You get very used to looking for the reflection of a window or the lack of reflection from an open window. After doing security on and off since I was 21 it was quite ingrained in me and therefore I could concentrate on watching what Hooch was telling me.

When you were walking around at night and through the forest you put your complete faith in your dog. You don't have the senses he has and can never pick up what he does. Dogs have instincts but they are very quickly backed up by their incredible senses. We have senses but all we can rely on is gut feeling a lot of the time. If something didn't look right or sound right or smell right it needed looking into.

The minute you pull your dog over to investigate something they know. It's amazing; it really is like they are telepathic. You get nervous; they instantly are on guard themselves. One of the greatest and easiest bits of training to do with a protection dog is to just stop and look around as if you've heard or seen something. Watch your dog; they go straight into guard mode. I swear it is like an insult to them that you heard something first.

It is similar to when you are out with your friend or your kids just shush them and watch them go into overdrive trying to hear what you've heard. Best to do it at night if you want to really freak them out.

I can't even remember who told me this but someone said to me to never look behind you on a night shift. *"If you do, you'll be looking behind you for the rest of the night."* I am not a superstitious or nervous man so I thought I would try it one night. Oh my god. I have never been so freaked out. All night I was looking over my shoulder. I decided from that night on that if someone was silly enough to creep up on Hooch and I, I would leave it to Hooch to look behind. Of course he never did, maybe it does the same to dogs.

After a few of these surprise attacks by Keith over the space of a couple of months Hooch was really into Wellington too. Always on the ball. He would notice things long before I did. It gave me a lot of faith in him and lets you relax and let him do the work.

I trained him to kennel guard as they call it. It basically means anyone comes near his space while we are at work he barks up. This is a great bit of training. When you are sat in your van eating your lunch or reading, you're really only looking forward. Practically it's tricky to look in your mirror into the pitch black abyss and pick anything out. So while Hooch was resting he would have the tailgate open, though he was resting he would pick up on anyone walking behind the van and very aggressively remind them he was watching them. It usually ended up in my tea down my front but it was handy in some cases.

When I knew we had really turned a corner was when we were walking around one night, we were on the kilometre and Hooch ears went forward, they don't go up. His posture changed and he started pushing me across to the right where there were bushes lining the road. His breathing became sharp and shallow, the grumble began and out from the bush jumped Keith, lively and fun not aggressive.

Let Hooch have a play on the sleeve and let him win. No barking or aggressive stuff. The idea we had discussed was if Hooch ever indicated he was to have a fun game, win and then go back to patrolling. It was a reward thing rather than a threat. I wanted Hooch to know that to indicate was good. In the same vain as detection dogs work for reward. I wanted their to be a difference for him so he indicates rather than reacts, it's much easier to manage.

It was a great workout for him, like I have said. With dog training you only need one time doing it right and you then just reinforce.

It reminds me of a great anecdote. I knew a gent that worked on the civilian side of the MOD dog handlers looking after sites around Surrey. He said to me once when we were talking about dogs. "*Have you heard of the GSD arc*" I shook my head, this was a new one on me. "*When you are patrolling*" he said "*if the dog indicates, his ears come up.*" This is mainly true. "*you get down to his height and look from behind his head, through his ears and down his nose. It will show you exactly what he is indicating at*" I didn't quite know what to say. You would assume that a dog would turn its head to where it's looking. I think bending down and using him like a rifle sight is a bit over the top when you can just look the way he is looking. It was a shrug your shoulders moment.

161

There are many times I have been confronted with amazing stories about dogs. I actually worked with a dog handler once that told me dogs couldn't look up. When he told me, I had Hooch next to me and I looked down to Hooch and he looked back at me with those adoring eyes of his and I said nothing. Not really much you can say to that.

The myths and rumours of what dogs can and can't do are endless. I think you can dispel most with a cursory look at a dog book or the internet or your dog.

The sixth sense rumour I actually have a bit of belief in. Only because the dogs I have worked have done things to make me belief in a truth about this. I am not frightened or worried about the spirit world, I believe in it more than I disbelieve it. I've never seen a ghost or an apparition but my logic is that I have worked at night for many many years in houses with huge histories, Henry VIII hunting lodge, churches and graveyards, old manor houses that contain a bucket load of stories of murdered stable boys and beaten maids that roam corridors and areas of garden. Never seen one, but more to the point. Never been hurt by one. If they wanted to, I would have been had by now. I have had moments of inexplicable activity.

I worked at a lovely manor house for a family that were worried because they were out in the sticks a bit. You could walk past the outdoor pool and sometimes you could smell lavender and a candle would be lit, I would blow it out and lo and behold next patrol it would be lit again. This was replicated for other Dog Handlers on that site. It was quite a regular occurrence.

The worst occasion of this was of a crypt we used to have to check was locked and not tinkered with at night. There were probably about 20 steps down under the church and round a corner to the door. It was dark and a bit spooky. I guess just because of what it was. I had been checking this door 5 or 6 nights a week for a couple of years. I went to walk down there with Hooch and he got down a couple of steps and stopped. I went down another to couple to try and coax him on. He wouldn't have it. It was not like Hooch to be stubborn about walking. He wouldn't move. I started pulling him, he eventually moved but only to place himself between me and the rest of the steps. At that point I took his advice and wandered back up, happy that the crypt could go unchecked for a night. That did freak me out. The following night and every night thereafter Hooch wandered down those steps unchecked. I was happy with my decision.

.

This was taken at the college by another Dog Handler

Nature Of the Beast

I was lucky enough to really forge myself a place at the College, became a part of the furniture and really got to know the staff and many of the kids. I loved working there. There was always something new and different to deal with and not too much trouble. There was more fun chasing kids about on special events where they traditionally sneaked out of their dorms and planted fir trees in the middle of the rugby pitch or covered statues with toilet rolls.

It took a bit of time but we got hold of it. You couldn't stop it because it was tradition and part of the tradition was the cat and mouse games between security and kids.

There were fireworks nights, proms, rugby matches. It was a great time.

Many of the sites I had worked were very solitary. Looking after a property for a family where you may or not get a bit of interaction from them but a lot of the time you were just the bloke in the van at the end of the drive.

By now I had worked for a few famous people and at some beautiful residences. I was really enjoying the job because it gave me so much time for training and just to be around my boy teaching him new stuff and with so much time you could really crack training. As long as it was training you could do on your own.

The College were relying on us a lot for many different remits and the hours were going up so I brought Keith in to work with us.

At this time I was working less on the dogs and doing more admin for the company. I would work a few shifts and then spend a couple of days vetting people and organising rosters.

We had a couple of regular guys working for us filling in shifts. The biggest problem with Dog Handling is because it wasn't regulated it was difficult to find the right calibre of people. With the right skills and the right license.

When I brought Keith in I knew he would be a great addition. I had worked with him before and he had always been reliable and trustworthy. He kept himself to himself and didn't get involved in gossip. This was an asset because there was a lot of gossip. So with my new role as a manager of the company I wanted to really make the company stand head and shoulders above all the others I had experience of.

I had this conversation with many of my colleagues and had always been dubious about setting my own company up. The reason for this was I didn't trust anyone to do the right thing. I had worked for many companies that started with the idea of really doing it right and all without exception had failed in their initial and overriding ambition to get it right.

I didn't want to do this; in fact I didn't even want to try. Such was the strength of my belief in the ultimate failure of the task.

Years prior myself and Keith had been offered a contract and we had both decided to turn it down because this is my belief. Working on these sites you would get people phone in sick or go on holiday and you would get a relief guy. He would turn up in a van with a blow up bed in the back or one guy turned up once in a Peugeot 106 and a collie. Such is the standard for many of these so called dog handlers. My point is this. One day someone will go sick or I won't be able to cover them. I will have to stoop to these lows to cover the site.

To me this was inevitable and at that point I become one of those security companies I moaned about to my friends. At that point I become that hypocrite. Though my principles may well keep my poor they are my principles.

I was steadfast in this belief and it doesn't seem to matter what is in the heart of the person who sets that company up. It will always be that day that the owner or wages payer turns up and sees that person that you had no choice to put on your site and when he confronts you he can say "*you said you wouldn't do that. Quality Dog Handlers you said*" He would be right, I would have said that.

I wanted my own business doing what I loved but I couldn't promise anyone the standards would always be the standard I promised because sometimes it is out of your hands and to get cover I would have to put somebody on that I didn't want on. A jacket filler.

I worked for a nice company once. Had all of these ideas same as mine. I worked for her for a little bit and one night she called me and asked me if she could put a guy on with me to learn the site. She was looking to employ him. He needed a bit of training but he was essentially a nice guy with potential.

So the next night I was at work waiting for this man. A Nissan Micra pulls in and I go across to say hello. As I approached the car I realised I couldn't see through the windows. There was something obstructing and then I realised it was a dog. A big dog. The man got out of the car, he said hello and we had a chat. Then I realised he had two dogs in the back. I asked him what he had and it was father and son. An English Mastiff and a Cane Corso x English Mastiff. The dad was 13 stone the son was 8. In the back of a Micra with the seats down.

It was ridiculous, I asked him to get them out and he got them out. They were lovely dogs, well looked after and friendly. I asked if he had any done any training in preparation for his break into dog handling and he said "*yeah I've done some bite work with dad.*"

"oh great I said. Let's see" So we put son in the cabin and walked to a grassy area with dad. I said *"ok what do I need to do to see him work."* He was stood with the hulk of a dog and looked confused. *"What do you mean"* he said. *"Do I need a sleeve? Is he going to bark up?"*

He walked across to a tree with this dog, *"watch this"* he said a word which apparently was out of the Jungle Book because he had trained his dogs to react to the words the elephants used in Jungle Book. As he said the word, the dog lazily walked to a tree and started chewing on it.

During the night I spoke to him seriously about how he would have to get different dogs if he wanted to work dogs. There is a point with dogs where they go from big scary to big cumbersome. This dog was big cumbersome and the son fell asleep while I was trying to wind him up. Like I say he loved these dogs and they were in great condition and very attentive to him so obviously well loved. They were never going to be protection dogs. I told him the only way to be a Dog Handler would be to go and get a GSD or a Mali and have it purely for work. He said he wanted to show the world what mastiffs could do.

Now let me clear this up if I may. I have no issues with mastiffs. I think they are great dogs and as a protection dog, well I wouldn't want to be on the wrong side of one. They are loyal, powerful and a lovely dog. But, There is also a reason people don't work them. The GSD is the most popular; it is like the Ford Mondeo of working dogs. Easy to train, powerful, agile, can be aggressive. They are like a jack of all trades. Mastiffs just aren't.

So in short this was the reason I had never set up on my own. But now I had the chance of setting the company I wanted but without the risk to my reputation and it seemed as though the boss wanted these standards too.

I believe if you can always work with like-minded people you have cracked one of the many riddles of working within a team and you are a little bit closer to having a happy work place.

It is very difficult to work with people who have different standards or objectives.

When I started working at the College the company which would become a large part of my life over the next five years was very small. In fact it was me, another Dog Handler and the owner.

With me doing less and less dog work. I was only working on site a few nights a week as we had now secured another site and had events to do, Keith and a couple of other lads were busy doing most of the shifts. It was now down to me to check up on site and make sure all the paper work was done like site checks and making sure the sites were covered.

I was enjoying the idea that I was a part of building this company. My experience and knowledge was being used and my knowledge was also being developed by having to read up and formulate audits to make sure the health and safety of the site was properly documented and all the procedures were clear and staff were trained in them.

The decision had been made that we were going to build a great company with quality staff, specialising in Dog Security but covering all aspects of manned guarding and Close protection. Events, static sites, offices. He wanted prestigious.

Most importantly we wanted a staff base to pick from so we wouldn't have the problem I have previously explained. I don't believe you can eliminate it but I believe you can cut the risk of it ever happening.

So what I believed to be a job was turning into a chance to build the business I had wanted but without the risk, also without the reward but hopefully I have taught you one thing and that is values differs for everyone. For me to be part of building a successful, quality business meant more than a monetary reward. And so it began.

I was missing Dog handling and the freedom that came from working with Hooch and working nights.

I now had to structure my days around getting Hooch enough exercise and still stimulating his mind.

I believe it is hugely important to keep your dogs mind busy. You must know the saying *"the devil makes work for idle hands."* It is no different for dogs. A lot of the problems with dogs chewing and making a nuisance of themselves is due to a lack of stimulation. Just like people you can have a day of hard physical labour and still go to bed and your mind can be whizzing around. The reason for this is you must tire yourself out physically and mentally.

It is the same for dogs take them up the park and run them with a ball for as long as you like but if you don't tire their minds you will have the same problems.

My worry was without working he would become bored and possibly start misbehaving. Dogs don't need a huge amount of stimulation depending on the breed but they all need some if you feel it is important to enrich their lives which I believe just like us, this will help with a happy and therefore healthy dog.

My plan was to start training with some of the staff. A free training session every couple of weeks would tick a few boxes.

It would bring the green dogs up to a standard where I would feel our duty of care as an employer was fulfilled. i.e. the dogs would protect the owners so we would have confidence in the guys walking around on their own at night and happy that they would be safe with their dogs protecting them.

It would empower the staff; there were very few security companies that offered free dog training. Showing staff you value them and giving the dogs a good run out and some fun to enhance their lives too.

It would also give me the chance to continue Hooch's training and keep him sharp.

As a company we could keep a check on who was making the grade and taking the role seriously. Ignite the passion of dog training and working under the new starters as and when they were working for us. Some people thoroughly enjoy the competition, or just the knowledge that comes with learning how to work them.

As I said earlier in the book. It took a while for me to find a good dog trainer and all the things that came with training alongside like-minded people. Where to get equipment from, little problems solved, which food to buy and where to buy it.

My idea was to facilitate team training where our staff would get all of this in one place and reinforced every couple of weeks. It was and still is important to me to keep peoples interest in whatever you do. Jobs can become mundane very easily and walking around in the cold and wet was no different. But if you can keep peoples passion high and show them the end result by having experienced dogs at training to. It may well be the lure that our staff needed.

There was an added advantage of team building and having a bit of banter with friends. Also staff could invite friends and maybe this could become something else we could offer as a company and my dream would come true of just training people and their dogs for a living.

Before our first training session I had an interview booked. The interview was to bring someone else in to allow me more time to structure the company.

I was interviewing a guy named Ryan, he had sent his C.V. over and though he had no relevant job experience, he did have experience with dogs. He would be completely green to working dogs but at the interview his enthusiasm shined through. I had no idea then that he would become and remain a good friend.

He was interested to work for us, from everything I had said and all the things I told him about the company. How we valued our staff and really looked to train our staff up to a great level.

He accepted the offered job but didn't have a dog. I did a bit of digging about and a guy I used to train with had a GSD named Colt for us to look at.

Ryan and I had to drive to Northampton. I thought it would be a good idea to get to know him a bit better also with all due respect to Ryan he had little idea as to what he was looking for.

I am not sure whether it is working with dogs for a few years or I have a natural affinity but I can look into a dogs eyes and get a reasonably accurate reading. When you are looking for dogs to work you need this. It is the same as seeing the potential in people. A bit like Ryan in fact. He may have had no experience in Dog Handling you could tell he had potential and would learn quickly. With the added advantage of his love for animals and his sense of humour, I was 100% with the right support he would learn as much as he could and was without a doubt one of those people who would never do anything half arsed.

Dogs are similar. You can meet a dog that has no experience and maybe even lacks confidence but you can see in his eyes that he would do it, wants to do it. Hooch was one of these and now I was in Northampton trying to find the same attributes in a dog for Ryan.

As I have previously said. I wanted the company to be right from the bottom up. I had Keith in place and now was looking for other people to come in and really show the college that Dog Handlers could do customer service and people facing events. So far they had only known dog handlers. I wanted to show them that we could add value to the security provision by being approachable and professional with dogs that could be approached and had calm heads but could also do the business so it was hugely important for me to find a dog that matched Ryan's passion to learn and could grow with him.

I decided it would be more beneficial for Ryan to have a green dog with the right temperament and the want to learn and learn fast. It was also massively important to get a nice dog. Teeth on a lead would not work. Ryan had a wife and two young kids. The dog had to be of sound mind and calm persuasion.

So with a small mental list of things to look out for we went and looked at Luke's dogs.

Luke and I had had been in Dog Handling for a few years, we had been at training together at times and worked similar sites. He had now set up a small company. The company trained protection dogs and sub contracted some work out to Dog Handlers. Also they had a dog boarding and walking service. It was a nice little company and Luke and his wife worked hard to keep it so. With a young family it was no mean feat. I was confident in getting a good dog from Luke it was just finding the right one for Ryan. Like people you have to make sure it works.

The connection between dog and handler is key in all of this. It is so important for the dog to connect and vice versa. It is even ok to have nonchalance, usually from the dog. If a person wants to work with dogs you will generally get a good response from the person but there must be a response from both.

Dogs will very quickly let you know if they are not comfortable with the handler. Dogs judge very quickly, they've had to, that's nature. They rarely change their mind either.

Added to the small mental list of attributes I had, equally as important was the bond. If you are lucky handler meets dog, dog likes handler, handler likes dog. All good.

Not quite as good but still ok is handler meets dog, dog couldn't care less, handler likes dog.

Obviously there are many variations. Utopia is the dog choosing the person and the person being happy with that. When I met Hooch there was an instant bond, like when you meet a mate of a mate or a work colleague for the first time and you just know you will get on. Dogs have the same reaction except for a dog it is stronger, more pure. I don't know why but they like you and that is it. They bond to you and if you are a leader in their eyes they will instantly look to you for leadership.

This is how dynamic dogs are, if their leader gets injured in the hunt, the next leader takes over. Milliseconds, with no discussion, vote or anything else. It just happens, when they stop hunting they may find challengers but right then it's the good of the pack. The hunt is all that matters.

If a dog is nonchalant it can be won around in time, it isn't the perfect scenario and on top of your training you now have to work hard to bond as well. But it's viable and sometimes the bonding takes less time than you may think it will. A dog has his own mind and won't be swayed easily but with the right tricks they'll learn. Like that bloke at work after a month or two you say "*I didn't like him at first, but he is ok*" Sometimes for a Dog Handler these bonds that are made the hard way can be the most fulfilling, another show of their skills and training methods with the dogs.

For Ryan I wanted an instant bond due to him having the dog at home with kids, if the dog has a bond with Ryan it won't spend too much time with the kids at first.

When dogs are first rehomed, this is a great time to bond with them. They are unsure of their surroundings making them a little bit insecure. If the dog has a bond with you they will stick to you because of this insecurity. You are now the only thing they know in this changed world. It may sound cruel but you cannot

170

do anything about their insecurity and you are bringing them into a home that is better than their last. The insecurity will be there whether you use it or not. You might as well use it. By being there be all and end all they develop a bond that is based on a trust whether it be false or not but the dog is trusting in you because it knows nothing else. If you can prove to the dog that nothing bad happens whilst in your presence the bond will grow stronger. You are now a crutch or a pillar of confidence for the dog to draw on. His own confidence will be built in time but for now he can draw from yours. This can increase the bond very quickly.

So Ryan and I went in for a chat with Luke and he showed us a few of his dogs. Many were just a bit too much for Ryan and his situation. They were nice dogs and would have made good working dogs if you had a kennel in the garden for them.

Ryan needed a family dog and though you can never be absolutely 100% you can look for dog that have less of a propensity to violence than some he was showing us.

We went to the back and there was a small GSD, I say small because he was quite skinny. His name was Colt and I could tell Ryan was on it. I didn't know then but I do now, Ryan is quite impulsive.

After we spent a bit of time with him, Ryan was bonding well and Colt seemed happy with the match. It's funny looking back but then I felt as though as I was the one with the experience I channelled and managed the sale. Tried to keep Ryan's excitement down and to remain objective. But what I realise now is that Ryan was going home with Colt, I just didn't know him well enough to know that yet.

Ryan haggled a bit and we ended up taking him home. He was a lovely dog . Good natured, young, athletic and very quickly looked to Ryan. Even on the journey home he was already looking to Ryan.

Ryan does have a natural way with dogs, as I've said before I think dogs can tell good from bad. People that like them and people that don't. If you have a decent heart they will warm to you very quickly. I also truly believe that if you don't expect anything from them they will warm to you quicker. If you just want to be in the company of your dog because you want to be in the company of your dog that is when they are most comfortable with you. Neither of you have any expectations; you are just in that moment enjoying the peace that each of your presence bring to the other.

I am not a cat man, I like them, I admire them for their predatory instinct. But I like my dog because he depends more on me. Cats just do as they please. Cats always sit on me, they make a beeline for me. I think it is the same explanation.

171

People that know cats tell me this is because I am not a fan, they like to wind you up, or they want to change my mind. I don't believe this. I think it is for the same reason. I want nothing from them. Just their company and that peace you get when stroking a pet. It's simple and it suits them.

My Friends

If we should meet again on another street, I will gladly take up your fight.

I am a Working Dog and together we are guardians of the night.

I have been exceedingly lucky in my career and worked with some amazing people and some amazing dogs. Some of those dogs were mine and many were other peoples. I met many and learnt from them all. People and dogs are not as far apart as many would like to think.

I have learnt much more from watching not just people and not just dogs but watching the relationships, reaction and bonds between people and dogs. What works for dogs and what works for people have in my experience been linked and the only real difference is that dogs seem to have a much simpler way of thinking and a few less drives.

It is the few less drives that make them such a loyal companion to us. Dogs just want to be loved and nurtured. In a practical sense with food and shelter and in a deeper sense within the pack.

The poem that I have threaded through the book I have put in its entirety at the back. It is a beautiful poem and nobody knows who it is written by. Whoever it was has encapsulated all that being a Dog Handler meant to me and in their own little ways all of my dogs feature in this poem.

Hooch has been my friend and will always be. He is getting older and I know that one day I will have to promise to meet him again but while I have him here in this world he is my boy and there was a time a when we were unpassable.

This book is about the time before then, during then and after. It is about the bond you have to build with your dog, your friend or your child that makes all of the future so much easier for them and for you. For discipline and for praise. For learning and for experiencing.

It is so important you lay these foundations and do them with respect and with dignity not with aggression and fear. You will only form and help a dog or a person to grow into a great dog or person if you show them belief and leadership.

Hooch is without a doubt a shining example of what can be achieved with this approach and whether I did it right or wrong technically it doesn't matter because Hooch knew what I was doing was for the right reasons and that is all that matters to them. They follow when they know what is happening and what is being trained is for the good of the pack.

Hooch knew and still knows that what I do I do for the pack, he knows his pack and he understands where everyone is.

It is not easy to explain what I am trying to get at in the book, I hope I have explained it well. The feelings are particularly difficult because I cannot name them or put a name to them.

I will tell you this, my dogs inspired me to write this book. My belief in their general goodness and that they enhance our lives will never change because I know 100% my dogs have changed mine and always for the better. When I have had a wobble or a moment, they have always been there and you can ask no more of anyone.

Where are we now

Hooch and I retired from Dog Handling August 2013. I took up a "normal" job and continued with my interest in dogs. I think once you have the bug you never get rid of it.

You probably want to hear more about Hooch than me, it's fine I am used to it.

This is Hooch and I last year 2016 at a beautiful place named Bewl Water

Hooch is ten and a half upon writing this book. He still has the energy and mind of a puppy with the bones of a senior dog. Unfortunately he has arthritis in his rear ankle. It troubles him but not enough to stop him running around like a lunatic if he sees another dog or if I growl at him.

This picture was taken shortly after his tenth birthday.

I hope that I age as well as he does. He can go for a good hour long walk and be charging the whole way, but when he gets home he flops and is done for the day.

How far the great have fallen, but I still have many great memories of the things that we did, against all odds.

The comments we used to get when we first started with training and the challenges we overcame and the people we showed that it isn't about breeding and getting the fashionable dog. It is about how you nurture them.

I don't think we will ever answer the nature vs nurture question but Hooch defied much of what people believed and we showed them you can just take a dog and physical attributes aside, turn them into a great protection dog.

Hooch became well known, not just for his size but he could walk into a training scenario and show Dog Handlers new and experienced exactly what calm and obedient dogs can do and how their temperament can change to teeth and spit and instantly back again with one word.

We did a display at a rifle club in Bisley in front of many military people and Hooch showed how he could attack and return, on lead and off lead. He has always been a showstopper because of his power but like I have said many times he has a calmness, an aura. But in the context of bite work and protection work he has a pride, a simmering power and his posture in this picture says it all. Hooch went on to do an amazing display and bit off lead and on lead. Went in when told to and came straight out when told to. The only problem was when he came out he decided to go into the crowd to say hello to everyone. All the spectators had met him because that was part of the show, the fact that he could be around and socialise and then do his job.

After the first time he wandered into the crowd he decided to do it the next time after the bite. He had a look on his face like he was enjoying it.

Such was the character of Hooch; he couldn't and still can't help being the clown.

This picture was taken at the display just before he decided to wander into the crowd for more fuss.

177

Guardians of the Night

Trust in me my friend for I am
your comrade.

I will protect you with my last breath, when all others have left you
and the loneliness of the night closes in, I will be at your side.

Together we will conquer all obstacles, and search out those who
might wish harm to
others.

All I ask of you is compassion, the caring touch
of your hands.

It is for you that I will unselfishly give my life and spend my nights
unrested.

Although our days together may be marked by the passing of the
seasons, know that each
day at your side is my reward.

My days are measured by the coming and going of your footsteps.

I anticipate them at every opening of the door. You are the voice of
caring when I
am ill.

The voice of authority when I've done wrong.

Do not chastise me unduly, for I am your right arm, the sword at your
side.

I attempt to do only what you bid of me.

I seek only to please you and remain
in your favour.

Together you and I shall experience a bond only others like us will understand when outsiders see us together, their envy will be measured by their
disdain.

I will quietly listen to you and pass no judgment, nor will your spoken words be repeated I will
remain ever silent, ever vigilant, ever loyal.

And when our time together is done and you move on in the world remember me with kind thoughts and tales, for a time we were unbeatable, nothing passed among us
undetected.

If we should meet again on another street I will gladly take up your fight, I am a Working Dog and together,

We are guardians of the night.

23841185R00101

Printed in Great Britain
by Amazon